KB033797

THE BOY
WHO LOST HIS FACE

LOUIS SACHAR

To Laura and Nancy,
for all you taught me

The Boy Who Lost His Face
Copyright © 1989 by Louis Sachar
All rights reserved.

This English edition was published by Longtail Books in 2014 by arrangement with
Louis Sachar c/o Trident Media Group, LLC, New York through KCC(Korea Copyright
Center Inc.), Seoul.

ISBN 979-11-91343-88-5   14740

Longtail Books

1

"SHE'S SO *ugly!*" **whisper**ed Roger.

Scott and Randy laughed.

David laughed too, even though he didn't think it was funny. Mrs. Bayfield wasn't ugly. She was just a lonely old lady who dressed kind of **weird**.

"Is someone there?" Mrs. Bayfield called out.

The smile left David's face. The boys **crouch**ed down behind the **bush**es next to the **rust**ed iron gate leading to her yard. They became very quiet.

Mrs. Bayfield was sitting in a rocking chair★ in front of her large though quite **dilapidated** three **story** house. She wore a yellow and white flowered dress and a red cardigan sweater. A **floppy** red hat covered her long gray hair. On her feet were red high-top sneakers✷ and purple knee socks. Her snake-head **cane**

★ rocking chair 앉은 채로 앞뒤로 흔들리는 의자.
✷ high-top sneakers 발목까지 올라오는 형태의 운동화.

lay across her **lap**.

They had come to steal her cane.

The cane was **carve**d to look like a snake **wrap**ped around a stick. The snake had two heads facing back to back. They formed the handle. **Embed**ded in each snake head were two sparkling green eyes. One of the heads had its mouth open, with a tiny gold tongue **stick**ing **out**.

"Look at her hair," said Scott. "I don't think she ever washes it."

The boys laughed, including David.

"I don't think she's ever taken a bath!" said Roger. "Have you ever smelled her?"

"I can smell her from here," said Scott, holding his nose. "She smells like a pig!"

Roger and Randy laughed, and again David laughed along with them, but not because he thought anything was funny. In fact, he liked the way Mrs. Bayfield smelled. He thought she smelled like Chinese tea.

He once stood behind her in line at the post office. The whole time he kept trying to **figure out** what that smell was, and finally decided it was like very sweet Chinese tea. That was also when he had gotten a good look at the cane.

He **knew better than to** tell Roger and Randy that he thought Mrs. Bayfield smelled like tea. It was one of those things that Scott would say was uncool.

"Okay, Scott," said Roger. "When I give the **signal**, you **grab** the cane. Randy and I will take care of Old Lady Buttfield."

"What do you want me to do?" asked David.

Roger didn't answer him. He just looked at David like he didn't know what David was doing there.

David didn't know what he was doing there either. He certainly didn't want to help steal a poor old woman's cane. Still, he felt disappointed not to be included in Roger's plans.

"You just be ready, David," said Randy. "Do whatever needs to be done."

David **nod**ded. He was glad that at least Randy was willing to include him.

"But be careful," **warn**ed Randy. "She's a **witch**." He smiled at David.

David smiled back, although he had no idea what he was smiling at.

"She stole her husband's face," said Randy. David **snicker**ed, but stopped **abrupt**ly when nobody else laughed. Scott **gave him a dirty look.**

"She waited until he was asleep," said Randy, "and then she **peel**ed it off his head. It's hanging on the wall of her living room. She talks to it."

"Weird!" said Scott.

"What happened to her husband?" asked David.

"He's dead now," said Randy. "But for a long time he just walked around without a face. He lived up there, in the **attic**, so nobody could see him."

David looked up at the window just below the **roof**. "Wow," he said. He wondered if Randy or anybody else really believed any of that **nonsense**. He knew Scott didn't. Scott couldn't.

Scott and David had been best friends since the second grade. Then, this year, Scott managed to **get in with** Roger and Randy.

"You're **hold**ing me **back**," Scott had told David. "If you want to **hang around with** Roger and Randy, you got to be cool."

"I'm cool," David told him.

"Well, just try to be cooler, okay?"

"I'm ice."

"What?"

"Never mind."

"See, that's what I mean," said Scott. "You say **stuff** like that around Roger or Randy and they'll think you're a **jerk**. And then they'll think I'm a jerk for being your friend."

Now David felt a little angry as he looked at Scott. Scott had talked him into coming along—to prove he was cool. But when they met up with Roger and Randy, Scott completely **ignore**d him. He made David feel like Scott's kid brother who just **tagged along**.

Roger stood up and pushed open the iron gate.

"Hello?" Mrs. Bayfield called out.

"Hello, there," replied Scott, entering the yard behind Roger.

David was the last one through the gate. He started to shut it, but Randy turned and whispered, "Leave it open."

The yard was **overgrown** with **weed**s except for a small **rectangular patch** of flowers in front of the **porch**.

6

"Good afternoon, boys," said Mrs. Bayfield from her rocking chair in the middle of the front yard. Next to her was a little table with a tall glass and a **pitcher**.

"Good afternoon," said Roger. "How are you today?"

"Quite well, thank you."

"Glad to hear it," said Roger. "My name is Frank. And this is George and Joe," he said, pointing to Randy and Scott. "And that's David," he said, pointing at David.

David's face **flush**ed.

"A pleasure," said Mrs. Bayfield. "I'm Felicia Bayfield."

David wasn't worried that Mrs. Bayfield knew his real name. As long as she didn't know his last name. It was just that Roger had done that on purpose.

"Would you boys like some lemonade?" asked Mrs. Bayfield.

"Why,★ thank you, Felicia," said Roger. "We just love lemonade. Don't we?"

"I love lemonade," said Randy.

David **shrug**ged. "Sure," he **mutter**ed, hoping that they'd change their minds and just drink the lemonade, then leave.

"Nothing like a cool glass of lemonade on a hot day," said Scott.

It wasn't a particularly hot day. They were all wearing jackets.

"There are some cups on the porch, if you would be so kind," said Felicia Bayfield.

Roger and Randy headed for the porch, directly behind Mrs.

★ why 오, 이런. 이유를 묻는 '왜'라는 의문사가 아니라 감탄사로 쓰였다.

Bayfield. David watched as they **stomp**ed through her small **flower bed**, **crush**ing the flowers. He smiled at Mrs. Bayfield, trying to show her that he really didn't mean her any harm.

"I hope the lemonade's not too **sour** for you," she said. "It's homemade."

"I like it sour," said David, still smiling. He watched Roger whisper something to Randy as they got some Styrofoam★ cups out of a plastic bag on top of an ice chest.✳

Roger returned with four cups and set them on the small table. "I'll pour," he said, and picked up the pitcher of lemonade.

Randy remained behind Felicia Bayfield.

"I hope there's enough," she said. Her eyes were bright green and sparkling like the green eyes on the snake-head cane resting on her lap.

Randy took hold of the back of the rocking chair with both hands.

"Oh, there's plenty," said Scott.

"Now!" shouted Roger.

Scott grabbed the cane while at the same time Randy pulled the rocking chair **all the way** over.

Mrs. Bayfield cried out as she fell on her back in the chair. Roger poured the pitcher of lemonade over her face, turning her cries into **sputter**s.

★ Styrofoam 스티로폼. 발포 스타이렌 수지를 일상적으로 이르는 말.
✳ ice chest 아이스박스. 얼음을 넣어 그 냉기로 음식물을 차게 보관하는 상자.

8

Her legs were sticking up in the air and pointed right at David. He found himself **staring** at the strangest **underpants** he'd ever seen—black-and-white-striped with red **ruffles**. They **extend**ed from above her waist down almost to her knees.

Roger **hurl**ed the empty pitcher at the porch. It **crash**ed through her front window.

"C'mon, David," **yell**ed Randy, standing by the gate. "Before she puts a **curse** on us!"

Mrs. Bayfield **slid** backward out of the chair. She **prop**ped herself up on her elbows and looked at David looking at her.

He wanted to help her or at least tell her he was sorry, but he didn't.

He **flip**ped **her off**.

Her green eyes **flash**ed at him. In an angry, **crackling** voice she shouted: "Your Doppelgänger* will **regurgitate** on your soul!"

David couldn't really get what she said, but he wasn't particularly worried about it. He didn't believe in witches or curses or any of those kinds of things. He never heard of a Doppelgänger.

Little did he know that someday his face would be hanging on her living room wall.

He ran toward the gate, which was now closed.

★ **Doppelganger** 독일어로 '이중으로 돌아다니는 사람'이라는 의미로, 자신과 똑같은 환영 또는 그 환영을 보는 것을 뜻한다.

2

ROGER WAS limping around on the snake-head cane. "Would you boys like some lemonade?" he asked in a crotchety old voice that sounded nothing like Mrs. Bayfield.

Scott and Randy laughed.

David hurried up behind them. "Whew," he said. "We did it!"

"All right!" said Randy. He held up his hand for David to slap.

David slapped at it but almost missed. Only his last two fingers hit Randy's hand. He'd never been very comfortable with high-fives.

"There are some cups on the porch, if you would be so kind," whined Roger. "I'd get them myself, but I'm too ugly!"

Randy and Scott laughed.

David smiled. "Well, I gotta go," he said with a half-shrug, half-wave. "Homework."

"Later," said Randy.

"Yeah, see ya, Ballinger," said Scott. For the last week or so Scott had only called David by his last name.

"Simpson," he **replied**.

David walked home feeling **miserable**. He felt worried, too. What if she called the police?

Well, at least he wasn't the one who pulled her rocking chair over. He didn't pour lemonade on her head. He didn't step on her flowers or break her window. He didn't steal her cane.

All he did was **flip her off**.

Really, when you think about it, what's so wrong with that? All he did was point his middle finger at her. What makes the middle finger any worse than any other finger? What if he had just pointed his **pinky** at her? That wouldn't have been a bad thing to do, would it?

As far as he could remember, he'd never **given anyone the finger** before, at least not for real. He remembered when he first learned about it in the third grade. He and Scott used to practice giving it to each other. It took a lot of practice to be able to do it quickly. They'd flip each other off all day in class, but only in fun. It was kind of like a game of tag.★ They'd **pretend** to scratch their nose, or the back of their neck, but they'd always be pointing their middle fingers at each other.

It was too bad that Scott had become friends with Roger and Randy. Actually Randy wasn't so bad. He would probably be a

---

★ game of tag 술래잡기.

good guy, thought David, if it wasn't for Roger.

But he knew the reason he had given Mrs. Bayfield the finger was to try to **impress** Roger. What do I care what Roger thinks? he asked himself. Except he did care, and he knew it.

"Hi, David!" his brother **greet**ed him when he got home.

"Hi, Rick," he **mutter**ed.

"You want to play a game or something?" Ricky asked.

"I got homework," said David. "I have to **memorize** the Gettysburg Address.★"

"We could just throw the ball around," suggested Ricky.

David smiled. "Sure. Okay."

Ricky's face **lit up**.

They threw the baseball back and forth in the backyard. In a way David felt like he was doing a good **deed** to **make up for** the bad deed he had done earlier. He knew how much Ricky looked up to him.

Ricky was in the fifth grade. Anything David did, Ricky wanted to do too. There was never an **argument** about what to watch on TV. Ricky wanted to watch whatever David wanted to watch. When David mentioned he liked a song on the radio, Ricky would go out and buy the record, saying it was by his favorite group. If David told Ricky a joke, he'd hear Ricky repeat it to his friends the next day, even if it wasn't all that funny.

★ **Gettysburg Address** 게티스버그 연설. 1863년 11월 19일, 미국 남북전쟁의 격전지인 펜실베이니아주 게티스버그에서 제16대 대통령 링컨이 전사한 장병들의 영혼을 위로한 연설.

David caught the ball and threw it back to his brother, who was using David's old baseball glove. David had given it to him at the end of last season. Ricky could **hardly** believe it. "Wow, this is the same glove you made that famous catch with," he had said. David didn't know what Ricky was talking about. "You know. Remember when you caught that hot **smash** and stepped on second base for a double play?★"

David had played second base. He was okay, but to hear Ricky tell it, he was a superstar. "They should put *you* at shortstop✻ instead of Scott," Ricky said.

Scott always seemed to be a little better than David at everything. Even his grades were better. That was something David couldn't understand. How could someone as smart as Scott **get along** so well **with idiot**s like Roger and Randy?

He threw the ball back to his brother. He wondered what Ricky would think of him if he knew what his life was really like. That he **hung around with** guys who didn't especially like him. That he helped steal a cane from a **defenseless** old lady.

What if she is still lying **helpless**ly on the ground? What if she can't walk at all without her cane?

He imagined her having to **drag** herself across the **overgrown** yard, up the wooden stairs to the porch, and into the house. And Roger broke her front window, so all over the floor there would probably be broken glass that she'd have to **crawl** across.

★ **double play** 야구에서 2명의 선수가 한꺼번에 아웃되는 플레이.
✻ **shortstop** 유격수. 야구에서, 2루와 3루 사이를 지키는 내야수.

The glass **pitcher** probably broke, too. She could be **bleed**ing to death at this very moment.

He tried not to think about it as he threw the ball back to Ricky.

She probably doesn't have any family or friends, he thought. She was so happy to see us, **delight**ed to have some visitors.

Or what if she does have a family? Will she be able to tell them what happened? Or will she just clean herself up and say nothing to anyone, because it's too **humiliating**? Maybe just pretend it never happened. "How did you break the window?" her son might ask. "Oh, you know **clumsy** old me," she'd answer, not wanting to talk about it.

David almost felt like crying. What if some kids did that to his own grandmother? Or to his mother, when she got old? Or to Elizabeth?

Elizabeth was his baby sister, who just had her first birthday.

Mrs. Bayfield was once one year old. She was once a cute baby girl whom everybody loved. Who would have thought then that someday she'd be a **crippled**, lonely old lady and some kids would **knock** her chair over, pour lemonade on her head, and steal her cane?

And then when she's lying helplessly on the ground, humiliated, unable to walk, without a friend in the world, some stupid kid flips her off.

He threw the ball hard, too hard, to his brother. He hadn't meant to throw it that hard.

Ricky caught it and **beam**ed. "Nice throw!"

14

David **sigh**ed as he considered going back to see her. He wanted to make sure she was all right. Maybe he could even be her friend. At least tell her he was sorry.

He wanted to go back, but he didn't.

What if Roger or Randy found out? He'd be the joke of the school. Besides, the police might be there waiting for him. *The criminal always returns to the scene of the crime.*

Ricky threw the ball as hard as he could. David had to jump and catch it backhanded.★ "Great catch!" said Ricky.

David started to throw the ball back to Ricky, but for **a split second**, instead of seeing his brother he saw the image of Mrs. Bayfield **tip**ped over in her rocking chair with her legs up in the air and her black-and-white-striped underwear with red **ruffle**s.

The ball **sail**ed high over his brother's head and way off to the left.

It **shatter**ed their parents' bedroom window.

★ **backhand** 백핸드. 테니스 등에서 쓰이는 용어로, 손등을 공 쪽으로 향하게 해서 치는 것을 말한다.

3

ELIZABETH said "ball."

It actually sounded more like "baw," but her mother knew what she meant. That was the reason David and Ricky didn't get in trouble for breaking the window.

Elizabeth and her mother were sitting on the bedroom floor at the foot of the bed, reading Elizabeth's favorite book.

"Mr. Duck and Mr. Goose Went for a ride on the red **caboose**."

"Gaboo!" said Elizabeth, her finger on the picture of the caboose.

At that moment the ball came **crash**ing through the window, **bounce**d and rolled across the bed, bounced on the floor, and landed in Elizabeth's **lap.**

"Baw," said Elizabeth as if it were a very common thing for a baseball to suddenly crash through the window and land in her lap. She picked it up and showed it to her mother.

It all happened so fast that by the time Mrs. Ballinger realized what had happened it was already clear that the danger was past and nobody was hurt. She just laughed.

"It was my fault," said David, **rush**ing into the room.

"I should have caught it," said Ricky, right beside him.

"You couldn't have caught that ball," said David.

"I could too," said Ricky.

Their mother and Elizabeth were laughing at each other.

"It's my fault," David repeated. "I'm the one who should get in trouble."

"No one is in trouble," their mother said. "Both of you please clean it up while I hold Elizabeth."

"But Elizabeth could have been hurt," said David.

His mother looked him right in the eye and said, "Yes, I know."

The broken glass was **confine**d to the bed.

David and Ricky folded up the ends of the **bedspread**.

Their mother read to Elizabeth, "Mr. Goose and Mr. Duck went for a ride on the green dump truck.★"

"Dum tugg!" said Elizabeth.

They lifted the bedspread off the bed.

"C'mon, Mr. Duck," said David.

"Okay, Mr. Goose," said Ricky.

IT DIDN'T seem right.

★ **dump truck** 차체를 기울여서 한꺼번에 짐을 내릴 수 있는 트럭.

I should have gotten in trouble, David thought. It was my fault. I broke the window. And Elizabeth could have gotten hurt. What if the ball hit her on the head or a piece of glass got in her eye?

Besides, what kind of lesson was that for Ricky? He has to learn **responsibility**. If you do something wrong, even if it's not on purpose, you still have to **suffer** the **consequences**.

I should have been **punished**, he thought.

4

SINCE THE second grade David had stopped by Scott's house every morning on the way to school.

Scott's mother answered the door with a cup of coffee in one hand and half a croissant★ hanging from her mouth. She looked at David like she was surprised to see him.

She pulled the croissant from her mouth. "Scott's already left, Davey," she said. "I **assumed** you were with him."

David shrugged. "No **big deal**," he said. Then, "Oh, that's right!" as if he suddenly remembered something. "Scott had something he had to do this morning."

Scott's mother had the coffee cup to her lips, and he walked away quickly before she had time to ask him anything more about what Scott had to do this morning. For some reason he felt **embarrass**ed in front of her, that her son hadn't waited for

---

★ croissant 크루아상. 초승달 모양의 빵.

him.

"Bye, Davey!" she called after him.

He waved with his back to her.

They had been Davey and Scotty until the fifth grade; then they became Dave and Scott. But Scott's mother still called him Davey. He called her Sally.

Once, when he was in the third grade, they had spent half an hour crying in each other's arms after they had seen a dog get run over by a jeep.★

It was kind of funny, he thought now as he walked away, that he called Scott's mother Sally but Scott he called Simpson.

When he got to school he saw Scott and Randy standing on either side of the door to the boys' bathroom. He headed toward them unsure if he was their friend, but they were right on the way to his locker and he didn't think he should have to go out of the way just to avoid them. Besides, he had helped them steal the cane. That proved he was their friend.

"Hi," he said.

"Hey, Dave, how ya doin'?" asked Randy.

"Ballinger," muttered Scott.

"Simpson," said David.

"So what was it that she said to you after you **gave her the bird**?" asked Randy.

"The bird?" asked David.

"You know," said Randy. Then, smiling, he gave David the

★ jeep 자동차의 네 바퀴를 모두 구동할 수 있는 소형 4륜 자동차 또는 그 상표명.

finger.

David had never heard it called the bird before. "I don't know," he said. "She was just **babbling**. I mean, she could **hardly** talk with lemonade coming out of her nose." He laughed.

Neither Scott nor Randy laughed.

"I don't know, man," said Randy. "It sounded like she put a **curse** on you."

David smiled. "Yeah, right," he said.

A boy with long **sloppy** hair and blue sunglasses **approach**ed the bathroom door.

Scott and Randy **immediately block**ed his **path**. "Bathroom's closed," said Scott.

The boy stood there a moment. David **recognize**d him from Spanish class. His name was Larry Clarksdale. He had only been at the school a few weeks.

Larry **chuckle**d as if it were some kind of a joke. "C'mon, let me through," he said.

Scott and Randy didn't **budge**.

"Can't you read the sign on the door?" asked Randy.

There was no sign on the door.

"It says, 'Closed for **Repairs**,'" said Scott.

Larry looked at David, or at least David thought he was looking at him. It was hard to tell where Larry was looking behind his blue sunglasses.

David shrugged.

Larry also shrugged, then turned and walked away, slowly at first, then very quickly.

Randy **snicker**ed.

"Go use the girls' bathroom, **pervert!**" Scott shouted after him.

A moment later Roger stepped out of the bathroom. He laughed when he saw David.

David couldn't tell if Roger was laughing at him or with him. He smiled.

"So, David, you want a smoke?" asked Randy. "We'll **stand guard.**"

For **a split second** David actually considered it. "Uh, no, thanks," he said. "Maybe later."

He saw the look of **disapproval** on Scott's face.

"What'd old Buttfield call you?" asked Roger. "A **pimple-banger?**★"

"I don't know," David said with a shrug. "I gave her the bird," he added, trying to sound tough.

"Big deal," **scoff**ed Roger. "She probably doesn't even know what it means!"

Randy and Scott laughed.

So did David, for **lack** of anything else to do.

DAVID'S HOMEROOM was a **combination** social studies and English class. He tried to put everything but the Gettysburg Address out of his mind as he looked it over one last time. Ricky had helped him **memorize** it. Ricky had been very

---

★ banger 돼지고기와 빵가루를 넣은 소시지.

22

impressed that David could memorize all those big words. But the big words were easy. It was the little words that were hard; all the "to's" and "for's" and "a's" and "the's."

Roger's voice suddenly **pop**ped into his head. *Big deal*, he had said. *She probably doesn't even know what it means!*

Roger had meant it as a **put-down**, but now as David thought about it, it made him feel better.

Maybe Mrs. Bayfield didn't know what it meant! If she didn't know what it meant, then it wasn't a bad thing for him to do. It would be no different than if he had pointed his elbow at her.

He wondered how long people had been giving the finger. Maybe they'd only been doing it a few years.

Who made it up? he wondered. Who decided it was a bad thing to do, and how did so many people find out about it?

He wondered if his parents knew what it meant. Maybe his father, he decided, but **definite**ly not his mother. How could she? Somebody would have had to show it to her and tell her what it meant, and he couldn't imagine that. And if his mother didn't know what it meant, then Mrs. Bayfield probably didn't either.

"Miss Williams," said Mr. MacFarland.

David felt a **pang**, just as if Mr. MacFarland had said "Mr. Ballinger."

"Are you prepared to **recite** the Gettysburg Address?" asked Mr. MacFarland.

"Except for the hat," said Miss Williams.

"I **beg** your pardon."

"Nothing."

A lot of the kids thought Miss Williams was **spacey**, but David knew what she meant. She was making a joke. It was like she needed to wear a stovepipe hat* in order to recite Lincoln's Gettysburg Address.

She stood up. "Should I say it here, or do you want me to go to the front of the room?"

"Wherever you feel most comfortable, Miss Williams," said Mr. MacFarland.

Miss Williams remained at her desk, standing very straight. She had long red hair, bright green eyes, and, thought David, just the right number of **freckles**.

He didn't know how many freckles she had, but he knew it was just the right amount. He sometimes **daydream**ed about sitting beside her in a beautiful **meadow** and just **count**ing her freckles.

He was glad that Mr. MacFarland had called on her, so he could stare at her without having to worry about being caught. He sat two rows to the left of her and one row back. If the classroom was a chessboard, he was a knight's* move away from her. If she was a queen and he was a knight, he could **take her off** on his next move.

She took a deep breath and began: "**Fourscore** and seven

★ stovepipe hat 약 18cm정도의 높이의 실크 해트.

✱ knight 체스의 나이트. 기병을 나타내며 말의 머리 형태를 하고 있다. 두 칸 전진 후 전진한 방향에서 오른쪽 또는 왼쪽으로 한 칸을 이동할 수 있다.

24

years ago our—"

"Stop!" **command**ed Mr. MacFarland.

She **stared** bravely at the teacher.

"Miss Williams, do you know what 'Fourscore and seven years ago' means?" he asked her.

"No," she said very quietly.

"No," he repeated. "Tell me this. How long did it take you to memorize Lincoln's Gettysburg Address?"

"I don't know, about an hour."

"You mean to tell me that you spent all that time saying the words, over and over again, and you don't even know what they mean. Are you a robot?"

She pushed out one side of her face with her tongue.

"Do you own a dictionary, Miss Williams?"

"Yes."

"Didn't it ever **occur** to you to look up the words in the dictionary?"

"I know what they mean separately," she said. "Just not together."

Mr. MacFarland turned toward the rest of the class. "Will someone please tell Miss Williams what the words mean *together*."

Several kids raised their hands. David didn't. He knew what "fourscore and seven" meant, but he wasn't about to show her up.

"Mr. Schwartz."

Jeremy Schwartz explained that a score was twenty, so that

fourscore and seven **equal**ed eighty-seven.

"Thank you," said Mr. MacFarland. "Now tell us, Mr. Schwartz, why didn't Lincoln just say eighty seven? Why did he have to make it so **complicated**?"

"Maybe that's just how people talked back then."

"No, people said eighty-seven, just as they do today." He turned back to Miss Williams, who was still standing. "Miss Williams, why do you think he said fourscore and seven instead of eighty-seven?"

"Because it sounds good," she said **meek**ly.

"Because it sounds good?" Mr. MacFarland repeated. Several kids snickered. "What do you mean, it *sounds* good."

"It sort of **rhyme**s."

There were more snickers. David could hardly watch. He hated to see her **ridicule**d in front of the whole class.

"Do you mean to say," continued Mr. MacFarland, "that on the **site** of the **bloodiest battlefield** in the Civil War, where there were more than forty thousand **casualties**, where brothers killed brothers, President Lincoln chose those words because they *rhymed?*"

Miss William's face **quiver**ed.

Mr. MacFarland smiled. "Well, you're absolutely correct," he said.

David smiled.

"The Gettysburg Address is more than just a speech," Mr. MacFarland told the class. "It is a piece of **literature**. It is a **poem honor**ing the forty thousand young men killed or **wound**ed.

26

Mr. Lincoln came to that **horrible** site and spoke with **dignity** and **grace**. And now, Miss Williams, I'd like you to do the same. Recite the Gettysburg Address, but don't just say the words. *Feel* them. Imagine you're standing on that battlefield and speak with the dignity and grace **befit**ting the **occasion**." He smiled at her. "And you don't even need a hat."

Miss Williams smiled **sheepish**ly. Then with her head held high and her green eyes **flash**ing she spoke. "Fourscore and seven years ago, our fathers brought forth on this **continent** a new nation, **conceive**d in **liberty** and **dedicate**d to the **proposition** that all men are created equal. Now we are engaged in a great civil war, testing . . . ."

David closed his eyes, **lean**ed back in his chair, and listened to her clear, brave voice.

". . . We have come to dedicate a **portion** of that field, as a final **resting-place** for those who here gave their lives that that nation might live. It is altogether **fitting** and **proper** that we do this."

He opened his eyes to look at her again, but for a split second instead of Miss Williams he saw the face of Felicia Bayfield.

He **toppled** over in his chair.

Miss Williams stopped reciting. Several kids were laughing.

"Stay where you are, Mr. Ballinger," ordered Mr. MacFarland.

"Huh?"

"Maybe this will teach you to sit like a human being. Please continue, Miss Williams."

David felt like a bug as he lay on his back with his legs in the air while Miss Williams continued to recite.

"But, **in a** larger **sense**, we can not dedicate—we can not consecrate—we can not **hallow**—this ground. The brave men, living and dead, who . . . ."

David wondered if Mr. MacFarland knew what it meant to give someone the finger. He wondered if President Lincoln ever **flipped anyone off**.

". . . that these dead shall not have died in **vain**—that this nation, under God, shall have a new birth of freedom—and that government of the people, by the people, for the people, shall not **perish** from the earth."

5

AT **RECESS** David **hung out** with Scott, Roger, Randy, and some other kids, including two girls—Leslie Gilroy and Ginger Rice. Even though he was just **barely** part of the group, it still felt good to be hanging out with the two most popular girls in the school. He sat on the edge of a **planter** with a fake smile **plaster**ed across his face.

Roger told the others how they had **swipe**d Mrs. Bayfield's snake cane.

"Her name's Felicia!" said Scott. "Can you believe it? Felicia?"

They all laughed.

"Don't get too close to David," **warn**ed Roger. "She put a curse on him."

"Really, David?" asked Ginger.

David smiled. "That's right," he said, trying to sound **mysterious**. "I'm cursed."

"Yuck," said Ginger.

After recess David had science. Science and math were his two best subjects. His father was a scientist. After science was shop.

Randy was in his shop* class. David waved and said hi to him as he walked past Randy's worktable.

Randy waved back and loudly called, "Hi, Dave!"

Another boy named Alvin **whisper**ed something to Randy, then they both laughed.

David continued on toward his table at the other side of the room.

At the beginning of the year everyone had to sign up for either home economics* or shop. There was no rule that boys had to take shop and girls had to take home ec. In fact, David shared his worktable with a girl.

But girls can **get away with** doing "boy" things a lot easier than boys can get away with doing "girl" things. Shop was David's worst subject. He would have liked to have taken home ec. He knew he'd have to know how to cook some day. But he could just imagine what the other kids would have called him if he had signed up for home ec.

He was making a cheese board* shaped like an apple. He had drawn a picture of it on his **draft**ing paper, and now, slowly and carefully, he was trying to copy that picture onto a piece of **maple** wood.

★ shop, home economics 학교의 교과목인 기술과 가정.
✻ cheese board 치즈를 함께 담아서 칼과 함께 내는 용기.

Wham!

David's pencil **slip**ped as the girl next to him hammered a **nail** into the doghouse she was building.

David turned and watched her. She was short and skinny, with very short, straight black hair that hung like a bowl over her head. Her name was Maureen, but everyone called her Mo.

Wham! Wham! Wham!

He was **fascinate**d by the way her skinny arms could **wield** the heavy hammer and **pound** in the nail **all the way**, with just three hits. The doghouse was almost bigger than she was.

He finished drawing the apple on his piece of wood. It didn't look the same as his drafting paper drawing, but that didn't matter. He knew he wouldn't be able to cut it out along the lines anyway.

Wearing gloves and safety goggles, he **cautious**ly **approach**ed the **jig saw**. He set the piece of wood on the metal plate and turned the switch. He tried to **maneuver** the wood so that the **vibrating vertical blade** stayed on the penciled outline of the apple. So far so good . . . perfect. "Nuts!"★

He had cut the apple out perfectly, except he followed the wrong line at the top and accidentally cut off the apple's **stem**. The stem was also supposed to be the handle of the cheese board.

Well, not all apples have stems, he **console**d himself.

★ **nuts** 형용사로 '미친', '제정신이 아닌' 이라는 의미가 있지만 여기에서는 짜증이 나서 내뱉은 감탄사로 쓰였다.

He returned to his worktable, took out his **sheet** of drafting paper, and erased the stem. He had learned early in the year that if he couldn't make the project look like the drawing, he'd make the drawing look like the project.

"Is that for your *girlfriend?*" asked Mo.

"Huh?" said David. "I don't know." He **shrug**ged. "Maybe." He was **flatter**ed that Mo would think he was the kind of guy who had a girlfriend.

"Are you going to **carve** your **initial**s in it?" she asked.

"Why would I do that?" he asked. "She knows who I am." Whoever she was.

"Isn't that what you're supposed to do with hearts?" asked Mo. She returned to her project. *Wham! Wham! Wham!*

He watched her **bang** another nail in the back of the doghouse, then **glance**d back down at his own **measly** project. It did look more like a heart than an apple.

He looked up to see Randy and Alvin coming his way. He **nod**ded to them.

"Hey, Mo," said Alvin, **ignoring** David. "Me and Randy were wondering something."

Mo looked at them **suspicious**ly. "What?" she asked, hammer in hand.

"Are you a boy or a girl?" asked Alvin.

He and Randy **crack**ed **up** laughing.

"**Buzz off**," said Mo.

"She's neither," said Randy. "She's a dog! Look, she's making a house for herself!"

They laughed again.

"Watch out, David," said Randy. "I don't know if she's had her **rabies** shot.★"

David smiled.

"How would you like a hammer up your **ass**?" asked Mo.

David turned red. He wasn't sure if she was **threaten**ing only Alvin and Randy or if she was including him too. He didn't **dare** look at her.

Alvin and Randy laughed and headed back to their table.

David stared down at his cheese board. He didn't breathe until he heard Mo **slam** another nail into her doghouse.

★ **rabies shot** 광견병 예방 접종.

6

"YOU SHOULD have taken the **cigarette** this morning," Scott told him as they walked home together after school. "You didn't have to smoke it. All you have to do is go into the bathroom, light it, and let it burn for a few minutes so the smoke gets in your hair. One cigarette won't kill you."

"No, but my parents might," said David.

Scott laughed.

David laughed along with him.

He was glad that they were still friends, at least as long as Roger wasn't around.

"Sorry I didn't wait for you this morning," said Scott. "It's not that I don't like you. I mean you're still my friend, it's just that, you know, it's not good for my **reputation**. I have to think of myself, too. You understand, right?"

"I guess," said David.

"I'm **taking a chance** even walking home with you now,"

said Scott. "But you're my friend."

"Thanks," said David. "It's not both of them, is it?" he asked. "I mean, I kind of get the feeling Randy thinks I'm okay. It's just that Roger won't give me a chance."

Scott shook his head. "Man, you got that **backwards**," he said. "Roger was saying that maybe you were kind of cool, now that there's a curse on you, but Randy thinks you're just a total dipshit.★"

"DID YOU say the Gettysburg Address?" asked Ricky.

"No, Mr. MacFarland didn't **call on me**."

"Too bad!" said Ricky. "I know you wouldn't have made any mistakes."

David shrugged.

"Can I hear it again?" Ricky asked.

Once more David **recite**d the Gettysburg Address for his brother. He remembered what Mr. MacFarland had said, and he did his best to speak with the **dignity** and **grace befit**ting the **occasion**.

"That's right," Ricky said when David was through. "You didn't miss a single word."

Ricky had **memorize**d it too.

"Now do you want to hear my address?" asked David.

"Okay," said Ricky.

"1411 Meadowbrook Lane," said David.

★ **dipshit** 굼벵이, 한심한 사람.

Ricky **crack**ed **up** laughing.

David shook his head in **amazement**. He wondered why Ricky didn't realize that if he was really such a **neat** guy he wouldn't be reciting the Gettysburg Address to his little brother. He'd be out with his friends or even with a girl. Only **nerd**s stay home and recite Lincoln's Gettysburg Address to their little brothers.

What would Ricky think if he knew my **so-called** friends thought I was a dipshit? Or that there was a girl I liked, but there was no way she would ever like me? And that while she was reciting the Gettysburg Address I fell over in my chair and then had to lie on my back like a bug?

"Hey, Mom," said Ricky as she walked by. "Do you want to hear David's address?"

Their mother walked into David's room with her finger on her lips. "Shh," she whispered. "I just **put** Elizabeth **down**."

She had medium length light brown hair and **hazel** eyes. She always looked **worn out** but at the same time **content**. Before Elizabeth was born she had worked for a consulting firm, doing **statistical analysis**. At first she was just going to take six weeks off, then three months, then six months, and now she still **occasionally** talked about going back to work.

"Do you want to hear David's address?" Ricky whispered. "It's really funny."

"All right."

"David, tell her your address," said Ricky.

David shrugged. "1411 Meadowbrook Lane."

Ricky cracked up laughing again.

Mrs. Ballinger smiled politely. She **obvious**ly didn't understand the joke, if that's what it was. "Ricky, you need to clean your room," she said.

David watched his little brother walk out the door, followed by his mother. "Hey, Mom," he said.

His mother stopped and turned back to look at him.

He flipped her off.

For a moment she didn't **react** at all. Then in a **strained** voice she said, "Don't move until your father gets home."

She walked out of his room, **slam**ming the door behind her.

A second later he heard Elizabeth crying. He looked down at his middle finger, which was still raised, and pointed it at himself.

7

DAVID DIDN'T think his mother actually meant "Don't move." She was just too upset to choose her words **properly**. He had to stay in his room until his father came home, but surely he was allowed to move.

Unfortunately his father sometimes didn't get home until almost midnight. He worked in a **lab** at the university and would get so **involved** with his **experiment**s that he'd forget all about time.

David didn't know exactly what his father did, except that he was sort of working on a **cure** for **cancer**, but not really. His father tried to explain his work to him, slowly and simply, but then he'd always get **carried away** and start talking real fast about cutting and **cloning** and **splicing** DNA **molecule**s. He could go on for half an hour before realizing that David had no idea what he was talking about. Then he'd just shrug and say, "I'm working on a cure for cancer."

But David had also heard his father say that the only way to get a government **grant** was to say he was working on a cure for cancer. True, he hoped his research might **eventually** lead to a discovery that might help lead to a cure for cancer, but that wasn't really the main thing.

Ricky brought David his dinner on a tray. "I'm not supposed to talk to you," he said. "I'm just supposed to give you your dinner, then go right back to the kitchen."

"Okay," said David, lying on top of his bed.

Ricky set the tray on David's desk and started toward the door, then stopped and walked quickly to his brother. "What'd you do?" he whispered.

David shook his head.

He was too **ashamed** to tell Ricky he had **given** their mother **the finger**, but once again he knew he had **impress**ed his little brother. Here he was, eating alone in his room because of some great and **mysterious** thing he had done.

Maybe I really am **cursed**, he thought, picking at his dinner. I've got no friends. My mother hates me.

In an **odd** way it made him feel better to **pretend** to believe Mrs. Bayfield put a curse on him. It gave him an excuse. It's not my fault I'm a dipshit. There's a curse on me.

The door opened. His father entered, took one look at him, and shook his head.

"I'm sorry," said David.

"Don't tell me," said his father, sitting on the bed. "Tell your mother." He wore **torn** jeans and a T-shirt. This was how he dressed for work, unless he had to meet with somebody from the government, and then he wore a suit and tie. He had very **curly** hair like David's, but his hairline was **receding**. He also had a **scraggly beard** and **mustache**.

"I didn't think she'd know what it meant," David tried to explain.

His father **stared** at him **incredulously**.

"Who told her what it meant?" David asked. "Did you?"

"No."

"Then how does she know? Somebody had to show it to her and then tell her what it meant."

"I suppose you're right."

"How'd she tell you what I did?" asked David. "What'd she call it?"

His father thought a moment. "She didn't call it anything. She said, 'David did this to me,' and then she showed me."

"Was she very good at it?" asked David.

"Good at it?"

"I mean, was she able to do it easily?"

His father smiled. "No, actually she had to use her other hand to **bend** her fingers into place."

"I just thought—I mean Mom seems so **pure** and **innocent** and everything. I didn't think she'd know what it meant."

"Well, that's not the point," said his father. "Even if she didn't know what it meant, that still wouldn't excuse your actions."

"Why not?" asked David. "If you give somebody the finger, and that person doesn't know what it means, then what makes

40

it bad?"

His father started to say something, then stopped and reconsidered. "That's a good point," he **remark**ed. "There's nothing **inherent**ly bad about it. It is only bad because everyone has agreed it's a bad thing to do. I suppose it could just as easily have been made to mean something good—like 'good luck.'"

"Or 'I love you,'" said David.

"Right," his father said. He smiled, but then his face turned serious again. "Even if your mother didn't know what it meant, you did. You weren't thinking 'good luck' or 'I love you.' You meant it as an **insult**."

"I didn't mean anything," said David. "I was just testing her to see if she knew what it meant. It was like an experiment."

His father appeared to **mull** that over.

"Who made it up?" asked David.

"I don't know."

"Someone had to," said David.

His father nodded. "I guess so," he said. "And then, when he gave people the finger, he'd have to explain what it meant. Otherwise no one would care."

"They might think he meant 'good luck' or 'I love you,'" said David.

His father laughed. "Right," he said. "And then those people would give other people the finger, and they'd have to explain it too. But now we live in a world where people have been cursing and insulting each other for so long that we can do it without having to **bother** to explain it." He smiled sadly. "Aren't we lucky?"

"I wonder how long people have been doing it," said David.

"Quite a while, I suppose, for everyone to know about it."

"Do you think Grandma and Grandpa know what it means?"

"I'm sure they do," said his father. "But I never *experimented* on them." He smiled.

So did David. "But what if there is one person who doesn't know what it means, and you do it to her—or him? Is it bad? Elizabeth doesn't know what it means. If I went into her room and **flip**ped **her off**, would that be bad?"

"I don't know. I know I wouldn't like it if I was taking her for a **stroll** and somebody came along and said, 'Hey, Elizabeth,' and then flipped her off." He thought a moment. "But would that be because he was **offend**ing Elizabeth or because he was offending me?"

"I guess Elizabeth'll find out what it means some day," said David. "Just like Mom. It seems so hard to believe. It's sad."

His father nodded. "Why don't you go **apologize** to your mother," he said.

David started toward the door.

"David," his father called to him.

He turned around.

His father flipped him off. "Good luck," he said.

David flipped off his father and said, "I love you."

David's mother was quite **delight**ed to find out it was just an experiment. She was **flatter**ed that David didn't think she'd know what it meant.

42

8

DAVID WASN'T going to stop by Scott's house Tuesday, but it was right on his way to school, and maybe Scott would be there.

He wasn't.

"I told him he should wait for you, Davey," said Scott's mother, "but he seemed to be in a hurry."

"That's okay," said David. "I **figure**d he wouldn't, but you know, I mean since I had to walk right by your house anyway, I **might as well**—"

"Oh, he forgot his lunch," said Scott's mother. "Would you mind bringing it to him?" She disappeared back into the house, then returned a moment later with a white paper **sack**.

David carried Scott's lunch **all the way** to school, where he saw Scott, Roger, Randy, and Alvin all laughing together. He dropped Scott's lunch into a **trash** can. After all, he didn't want to **ruin** Scott's **reputation**.

He got his books from his locker and headed toward his homeroom. Maybe Mrs. Bayfield really did put a curse on me, he thought. Except even if she was some kind of **witch**, she would have put a curse on Scott or Roger, not me. All I did was give her the finger.

And then I gave my mother the finger too, he realized. Maybe Mrs. Bayfield **somehow** made me do that.

A **weird** thought **pop**ped into his head. He had broken his parents' bedroom window too, just like Roger had broken a front window in Mrs. Bayfield's house.

And, he suddenly realized, he had fallen over backward in his chair in homeroom, just like Mrs. Bayfield when Randy pulled over her rocking chair.

He smiled at the strangeness of it all.

The smile left his face when he saw Miss Williams coming his way. Her red hair hung over a long yellow and purple sweatshirt. He hoped she hadn't thought that he was smiling at her.

Her green eyes **flash**ed at him. "Hi," she said.

His mouth went dry. "Hello, Miss Williams," he said, nearly **gag**ging on the words.

She pushed on through the door and made her way to her desk.

He hoped she hadn't seen him **blush**. He felt like an absolute fool as he went to his desk.

He couldn't believe that he had called her Miss Williams. So what if he didn't know her first name? He should have just said hi back to her. "Hi," she had said, cool and sweet. "Hello, Miss Williams," he replied, **nerd**y and **dumb**.

He felt himself blush again, just thinking about it. Well, it's not my fault—I'm cursed.

Mr. MacFarland was talking about John Wilkes Booth, a **prominent** actor who **assassinate**d Abraham Lincoln right in the middle of a performance. "For all we know, President Lincoln might have thought it was all part of the play, right up until the last moment, when Booth **fired** his **pistol**."

She did say hi to me, David realized. That was something. He wished he knew her first name. He wondered if he had ever heard it before. He went through every girl's name he could think of to see if one rang a bell. Alice Williams. Amy Williams. Betty Williams. Barbara Williams. Carol Williams. Cathy Williams. Debbie Williams. Donna Williams . . . . He made it all the way through Zelda Williams, but the only bell that rang was the one at the end of the **period**.

AT **RECESS** he saw Scott and Roger and everyone **hang**ing **out** on the steps. Roger was waving his arms, talking about something, and everyone else was laughing.

David **sigh**ed. He didn't know what Roger was saying, but he **doubt**ed it was very funny. Still, he knew if he was there, he would have laughed too.

Leslie Gilroy was wearing Roger's black vinyl jacket.★ That

★ vinyl jacket 염화 비닐 수지를 사용해서 만든 인조 가죽 재킷.

was one of the games they played. Whenever a girl wore a boy's jacket it meant she wasn't allowed to talk to another boy. Leslie wasn't even allowed to talk to Randy or Scott without first taking off the jacket.

Leslie had long, **silky**, beautiful **blond** hair that she was always complaining about. It seemed whenever she wasn't the center of **attention**, like when the guys were talking about sports, she'd suddenly say, "I hate my hair. It's too straight. I wish it was like yours, Ginger." Ginger had dark **frizzy** hair.

David opened his math book and started on his homework. If he didn't have any friends, at least he'd get his homework done so he'd have plenty of free time after school. He laughed at himself. Free time to do what? Play with my little brother and his friends?

"You have to go with me, Ginger!" he heard Leslie **exclaim**.

He **glance**d up to see Leslie and Ginger coming toward him. He looked back down at his book but continued to watch Leslie and Ginger **out of the corner of his eye**.

They stopped right in front of him. Leslie took off Roger's black jacket and handed it to Ginger. Now she was allowed to talk. She turned to David and said, "No girl will ever want to wear your jacket. You're the ugliest boy in the whole school."

She took the jacket from Ginger and put it back on. Then the two girls turned and walked quickly back to their friends.

"I said it!" David heard Leslie exclaim. "I said it right to his face!"

"He didn't do a thing," said Ginger. "He just sat there."

9

WHAT WAS I supposed to do? David was still thinking two and a half hours later as he changed into his gym clothes. Punch Leslie Gilroy in the face? What'd they expect? I'm not going to say, "No, I'm not ugly." That would have been worse.

Roger was in David's P.E. class. David was glad that Roger's locker was on the other side of the locker room. At least he could get dressed in peace.

He headed out to the soccer field. He was good at soccer. He was a pretty fast runner, but more than that, he had quick feet.

As the teams got ready he discovered he was playing against Roger's team. Of course Roger was playing **goalie**. Roger was too cool to play a position where he might get **sweat**y or **mess** up his hair.

David ran up and down the field kicking the ball, getting kicked in the **shin**s, falling down, and getting back up.

Roger **lean**ed on the side of the goal with his hands behind his head and watched. Whenever someone kicked the ball at the goal, Roger would **casually block** it, then pick it up and **boot** it **all the way** to the other end of the field.

Just one shot, hoped David as he wiped the sweat from his face. One clear shot to kick a goal past him. Or maybe just kick it right at him, as hard as he could, right into the middle of Roger Delbrook's **smug** face.

The ball **bounce**d free and David ran after it. He stopped it with the side of his foot. Someone **charge**d him. David tried to **dribble** around, but their legs **collide**d and they both fell to the ground.

The ball rolled **harmless**ly toward the goal. Roger picked it up and booted it high over David's head.

David pulled himself back to his feet. He leaned over, put his hands on his knees, and took a deep breath.

There was a blocked kick and the ball was rolling toward the sidelines.* He ran after it and managed to save it with the **heel** of his foot just before it went **foul**. Then, turning around, he saw there was no one between him and the goal.

Except Roger.

He dribbled down the field trying to go as fast as he could without losing control of the ball. People were closing in from all sides. He just needed to get a little closer.

He **tap**ped the ball too hard, **knock**ing it too far out in

---

★ sideline 사이드라인. 경기의 좌우측 한계선.

front of him, too close to Roger.

Roger came out after the ball. David continued to charge even though he knew Roger would get to it first.

Roger suddenly stopped. David thought he saw a look of panic on Roger's face as he backed up to **defend** the goal. Roger was still backing up with arms outstretched as David reached the ball.

He smiled, then kicked it as hard as he could.

He wasn't even close.

The ball **soar**ed high over the goal and rolled all the way to where the girls were playing volleyball.★

All **trace**s of panic were now gone from Roger's face. "Go get the ball, butthead," he said **scornful**ly.

David **chase**d after it. He was the one who kicked it, and he was closest to it, except for Roger, who **obvious**ly wasn't going to get it. He **jog**ged to the volleyball court.

He stopped. Miss Williams was holding the soccer ball. She had **freckle**s on her arms and legs, too. Up till now he hadn't even known she was in his P.E. class.

He stared at her with his mouth open and sweat **drip**ping down his face. Besides her blue shorts and white button-down shirt, she wore a green headband and red high-top sneakers.

She underhanded the soccer ball to him.

He **exhale**d. "Thanks," he said.

"You're welcome, *Mr. Ballinger.*" Her green eyes sparkled as

---

★ volley ball 배구.

she smiled at him.

He returned to the soccer game **elated**.

10

DAVID SPENT too long in the shower, thinking about Miss Williams, what she said to him, and the way she smiled. He could still picture her with her green headband, her blue shorts, and her red high-top sneakers. He felt a sudden **pang** of **remorse** as he remembered that Mrs. Bayfield was wearing red high-top sneakers too.

The bell rang while he was still getting dressed. He hurriedly tied his shoes, **stuff**ed his gym clothes into his locker, and headed for Spanish class, his last class of the day.

"*Buenos tardes*, Dah-veed," Mrs. Guiterrez **greet**ed him as he walked in late.

"*Buenos tardes, señora,*" he replied.

He was **struck** by the fact that in Spanish *tardes* means afternoon, whereas in English "**tardy**" means late. Even though Mrs. Guiterrez said good afternoon to him, he had the feeling that in her own way she was also telling him he was late.

"Dah-veed!" Mrs. Guiterrez **whisper**ed sharply. She **wiggle**d her finger at him, **gesturing** for him to come to her.

"What is it?" he asked as he made his way to the front of the room.

"Come here," she whispered, now gesturing with her whole hand.

He heard several kids **snicker**, so he smiled. Leslie Gilroy was in his Spanish class. He didn't look at her.

He **approach**ed Mrs. Guiterrez's desk. *"Si, señora,"* he said. He had heard rumors that Mrs. Guiterrez had once been a judge in El Salvador★ or Nicaragua✶ or someplace like that, and that she had to suddenly leave her home in the middle of the night to escape from the Sandinistas✳ or *Contras*✶ or somebody.

"Dah-veed," she said. "You are **oblige**d to, ah"—she **struggle**d to find the right English words—"raise your . . . ."

Her **bracelet**s **jingle**d as she moved her hand in a circle, searching for the word.

"What?" he asked. *"Qué pasa?"*

She smiled at his Spanish and continued moving her hand around in a circle. *"Cremallera,"* she said. *"Comprende?"*✶

He shook his head. He didn't know what a *cremallera* was. "I'll try not to be late again," he said.

★ El Salvador 엘살바도르. 중앙아메리카의 태평양 연안에 있는 공화국.
✶ Nicaragua 니카라과. 중앙아메리카의 중부에 있는 공화국.
✳ Sandinista 산디니스타 민족 해방 전선. 1961년에 결성된 니카라과의 무장 혁명 조직.
✶ Contra 콘트라 반군. 니카라과에서 혁명으로 탄생한 산디니스타 정권에 대항하던 반혁명 게릴라 세력.
✶ comprende 스페인어의 '이해하다.'

"No, no," she said. "*Cremallera* is down. You need to lift up."

"My grades are bad?" asked David. "I need to raise my grades?"

She looked through him. Suddenly her eyes **lit up** as she remembered the word. "Zeeper!★" she **exclaim**ed.

"Zeeper?" asked David, still not knowing what she was talking about. "I need to lift up my zeeper?"

Suddenly he turned bright red. As **inconspicuous**ly as possible, he zipped his **fly**.

"*Gracias,*✶" said Mrs. Guiterrez.

The class was **hysterical**.

He returned to his seat, trying not to look at anybody.

He wondered who saw. All they would have seen were his Jockey shorts. Big deal! He wondered if Leslie noticed. Of course, it didn't matter whether she did or didn't, he realized. She'd say she did.

Big deal. What did he care what Leslie or anyone else said about him?

When the bell finally rang, he walked quickly out of the room, but not so quick that he'd **draw** any more attention to himself.

Someone **tap**ped him on the shoulder. He turned around.

"You and your friends think you're so cool," said Larry Clarksdale behind his blue sunglasses. "But at least I don't walk around with my *cremallera* down."

David remembered how Scott and Randy had kept Larry

★ zeeper 지퍼(zipper)를 잘못 발음한 것.
✶ gracias 스페인어의 '감사합니다.'

from using the bathroom yesterday so Roger could have a smoke.

"And *you* call *me* a **pervert**," said Larry.

"I didn't call you a pervert," said David.

"Your friends did."

"They're not my friends," said David.

"They're not?"

"No."

"Oh," said Larry. "Well, I think they're a **bunch** of assholes.★"

David turned and headed toward his locker. As he made his way across the school he noticed that Larry was still walking beside him.

"No one could really see anything," said Larry. "You had your back to the class the whole time."

"Mrs. Guiterrez saw," said David.

"That doesn't **count**. She's from South America," said Larry.

"So?"

"It's different in South America. People walk around **naked** down there all the time."

"How do you know?"

"I used to live there, in Venezuela, when I was nine years old. I used to see naked people all the time, boys and girls." He **shrug**ged. "It was no big deal. You get used to it."

"You saw naked girls?" whispered David.

"Twenty-three," said Larry. "We lived in an American

★ asshole 원래는 '항문'이라는 뜻이지만 '멍청한 녀석'이라는 비속어로 쓰였다.

54

section where everyone was usually dressed, but we used to go for drives, and you'd see kids walking around naked until they were like thirteen or fourteen."

"Wow," David said.

Larry smiled. "I got pictures, too," he said.

"Really?" said David.

"Not all twenty-three," said Larry. "Only twelve. I had to **pretend** to my parents that I was taking pictures of **scenery** and stuff, but I was really taking pictures of naked girls."

David laughed.

"I was just a kid then," said Larry. "It's no big deal to me now. You know, once you've seen twenty-three naked girls it's no big deal."

"Yeah," David agreed as if he had also seen twenty-three naked girls before.

"I can bring the pictures tomorrow," said Larry, "if you want to see 'em."

David shrugged. "Sure," he said as if it were no big deal, like maybe he just wanted to see the pictures because he was interested in photography.

"Okay, I'll bring them tomorrow."

"Okay," said David.

"Well, see ya tomorrow," said Larry.

"Bye."

"Bye, David."

David put his Spanish book into his locker. He didn't have any books to bring home since he had already done all his homework.

He was halfway home when it struck him. *I saw Mrs. Bayfield's underpants.*

"I really am cursed," he said aloud. "Everything that happened to her keeps happening to me."

That's stupid, he thought. Mrs. Bayfield didn't do anything to him. He just forgot to zip his fly after P.E. because he was in such a hurry.

He didn't believe in **witchcraft**. He was, after all, going to be a scientist when he grew up. He knew that everything had a **logical** and **scientific explanation**. He didn't believe in curses or **astrology** or **fortune** cookies★ or any of that stuff.

True, some of the same things that happened to Mrs. Bayfield happened to him, but that was just a **coincidence**. In a world where so many things are happening to so many people all the time, coincidences are **bound** to happen **now and then**.

"Okay, just one more thing!" he said aloud, looking up at the sky and speaking to Mrs. Bayfield or God or the Devil, or to whoever was in **charge** of **curses**. "Just do one more bad thing to me and then I'll believe I'm cursed."

He waited a few seconds for a **lightning** bolt to strike him, or maybe a **pitcher** of lemonade to pour on his head.

Nothing happened.

He took two steps, then stopped. He smelled something.

He checked the bottom of his shoe. Sure enough, he had

★ fortune cookie 중국 음식점에서 식사 후에 나오는, 운수를 적은 종이가 들어있는 과자.

56

stepped in it.

He could see it on the **sidewalk** behind him, with his **footprint** right in it. He laughed. "That doesn't count," he said. "That's got nothing to do with Mrs. Bayfield. I've stepped in that stuff before." He looked up at the sky and shouted, "I've stepped in it lots of times!"

11

Doppelgänger: a **ghostly counterpart** of a living person.

THAT WAS the **definition** David found in *Webster's Ninth New **Collegiate** Dictionary*. He also looked up **regurgitate**. It seemed to be a nice way of saying "**throw up**."

He could now clearly **recall** the words Mrs. Bayfield had said to him. *Your Doppelgänger will regurgitate on your soul.* My ghostly counterpart will **puke** on my soul?

What is a ghostly counterpart of a living person?

He thought about everything that had happened to him: breaking the window, falling over in his chair, **flipping off** his mother, his **fly**.

Nobody else caused any of that to happen. Mrs. Bayfield didn't do anything to him. He did it all to himself.

Or maybe he didn't. Maybe it was his Doppelgänger?

Whatever was going on, it sure felt like someone was

throwing up on his soul.

12

MISS WILLIAMS wasn't paying **attention** to anything Mr. MacFarland was saying. She was drawing a picture. David couldn't see what she was drawing, but it must have been funny, because every once in a while she would stop, look at what she'd done, and **smirk**.

Whenever Mr. MacFarland looked at her, her head would **instant**ly **straighten** up and she would look directly back at him. But as soon as he turned away she would smirk and go on drawing.

David **anxious**ly looked at the clock. He knew exactly what he wanted to say to her. He just hoped he had the nerve to say it.

The bell rang. David remained in his seat while Miss Williams put her drawing in her folder. He waited for her to stand, then he stood up and started walking so that they both reached the door at the same time.

"Good morning, Miss Williams," he said without looking at her.

"And good morning to you, Mr. Ballinger," she replied.

LARRY WAS waiting at David's locker. "I got 'em," he said, tapping his jacket pocket. He looked like a **drug** dealer★ with his blue sunglasses and long un**comb**ed hair.

David looked around to make sure no one was watching. They walked around to the side of the building.

Larry had eleven photographs of naked girls. "I thought I had twelve," he said. "I don't know what happened to the other one."

"That's okay," said David. He **glance**d over his shoulder to make sure no one was around, then took the pictures from Larry.

The pictures were a little out of focus, since they were taken by a nine-year-old kid in a moving **automobile**, but he could **definite**ly tell they were pictures of **naked** girls. Most of the girls were pretty young, probably under seven years old, but there were a couple of girls who were at least fourteen or fifteen.

Besides the naked girls David could also see the conditions around them: the dirt and garbage and **broken-down** tar-paper✷ houses. He felt **disgust**ed with himself. These poor people couldn't **afford** clothes, and here he was getting his **kick**s by

---

★ **drug dealer** 마약 밀매상.
✷ **tar-paper** 타르 용지. 방수재로 이용한다.

looking at them.

Still, he kept looking.

There was one picture of a girl about nine years old playing with a little black-and-white dog. The girl had long **stringy** hair and was dirty from head to toe, but she had the happiest face he had ever seen. She looked like she was just laughing her head off.

"I guess she's about our age now, huh?" David asked.

"Yeah, I guess so," said Larry.

"I wonder what her name is," said David.

"Carmelita," said Larry.

"You know her?"

"No. That's just the name I made up for her. She looks like a Carmelita."

David **nod**ded. "I wonder what she's doing now," he said. "Do they go to school?"

"I don't know," said Larry. "Some do, some don't."

They both **stare**d at the picture.

"I hope she's still happy," said Larry.

"Yeah, me too," said David, although it **hardly** seemed possible. How could she still be happy, living in all that **poverty**? "They don't eat dogs, do they?" he asked.

"I don't think so," said Larry. "She probably still has the dog."

"Then maybe she's still happy," said David.

All of his own problems suddenly seemed **petty** and **insignificant** to him, especially his **so-called** curse.

"Sometimes I wish I could go back to Venezuela and find her," said Larry. "And maybe give her some money."

"Wouldn't that be great!" said David. "Or maybe even bring her back here to America. She could live at one of our houses and go to school with us. I wonder if she'd be allowed to keep her dog."

"I wouldn't even know how to find her," said Larry. He took the **stack** of pictures from David. "You want these?" he asked **abrupt**ly.

David shook his head.

Larry threw them in a **trash bin**, all except Carmelita, which he put back in his jacket pocket.

13

"IT'S NOT a heart," said David. "It's an apple. It's a cheese board in the shape of an apple." He **rub**bed the **sandpaper** around the rough edges of his project.

"Well, it looks like a heart," said Mo. She hammered a **nameplate** over the **entrance** to the doghouse. *Wham! Wham! Thud!* "Shit!★"

She jumped up and down with her **thumb** in her mouth.

"Did you hurt yourself?" asked David.

She took her thumb out of her mouth and shook it wildly. "No, it feels good," she said. "I love hitting myself with a hammer."

David smiled. "That's like the guy who kept **bang**ing his head against the wall, and somebody asked him why he did it, and he said, 'Because it feels good when I stop.'"

★ shit '똥'이라는 뜻이지만 여기에서는 짜증이 나서 내뱉은 감탄사로 쓰였다.

Mo stared at him. "Was that supposed to be a joke?" she asked.

David **shrug**ged.

He looked at the nameplate that Mo had hammered onto her doghouse. It was shaped like a large bone, and on it, in big black letters, it said KILLER.

He returned to **sand**ing his heart-shaped apple cheese board.

"Hey, David, where you been?"

It was Randy. He and Alvin were **lean**ing on the side of David's worktable.

David looked up at him. "Hi," he said **flat**ly.

"So where you been, buddy?" asked Randy. "How come you haven't been **hanging around**? Everybody's been wondering what happened to you."

"Yeah, right," David **mutter**ed.

"Especially Leslie," said Randy. He winked at David. "I think she likes you."

"That's right," said Alvin. "Today at **recess** she said, 'Where's David? He's so cute!'"

"I think it was when you walked into class with your zipper down," said Randy. "That's when she fell in love."

He and Alvin laughed.

"Leave me alone, all right?" said David.

"Hey, what's the matter?" asked Randy. "Don't you like her?"

"It's your **curly** hair," said Alvin. "She **goes for** guys with curly hair." He rubbed the top of David's head with his hand.

David pushed Alvin's arm away.

Alvin pushed him back.

"Hey, look, he made a heart for her," said Randy, picking up David's cheese board. "If you want, I'll give it to her for you at lunch."

"Give me that," said David, reaching for it.

Randy held the heart behind him. "Don't worry," he said. "I'll tell her it's from you. I'll write on it, 'To Leslie, with love, from David.'"

Mo **grab**bed the cheese board out of Randy's hand. "It's not a heart, assbite!" she said. "It's an apple."

Randy took a step toward her but thought better of it when she picked up her hammer.

"What's the matter, David?" asked Randy. "You need a girl to **protect** you?"

"Is she a girl?" asked Alvin.

"I don't know what *it* is," said Randy.

They walked away laughing.

Mo handed David his project.

"Thanks, Mo," he said.

"You just have to **stand up to** those assholes," she told him. "You can't let them **push you around**."

David shrugged. It was a lot easier for her to stand up to them than it was for him, he thought. They're not going to fight a girl.

"You know, it does look like an apple," said Mo. "I mean, now that I know what it is, it definitely looks like an apple."

"It was supposed to have a **stem**," David explained, "but I accidentally cut it off. It would have looked more like an apple if it had a stem."

"Oh, yeah, I can see that," Mo agreed. "But that's okay. It still looks like an apple. I mean, not all apples have stems."

David looked at the doghouse with the nameplate KILLER **nail**ed above the entrance. "So what kind of dog do you have?" he asked.

"What?" asked Mo. "Oh, this." She glanced at her project. "I don't have a dog."

14

SCIENCE **MADE SENSE.**

It was **logical**. It was **consistent**. If you dropped a rock, **gravity** would always cause it to fall down. It wouldn't sometimes fall up. If you combine two parts **hydrogen** with one part **oxygen**, you'll always get water. You won't sometimes get milk.

Maybe that's why it was David's favorite subject. Nothing else in his life seemed to make sense anymore.

"David, will you please **assist** me," asked Mr. Lugano, his science teacher.

Mr. Lugano often called on David to help out with **experiment**s. The **chemical**s could be dangerous and David could be trusted. Some of the other kids **instant**ly turned into mad scientists whenever they were asked to help in an experiment.

"Hey, Ballinger," Scott **whisper**ed as David walked by him on his way to the front of the room. "Your **fly**'s down."

David didn't look.

It was Friday, three days since he'd walked into Spanish class with his *cremallera* down. Every time Scott or his friends saw him, they told him to zip his fly. If he looked down, they'd laugh. If he didn't look down, they'd call him a **pervert** who liked to walk around with his pants unzipped, until at last he'd look. Then they'd all laugh.

David had the feeling that they would leave him alone if it wasn't for Scott. It was like Scott was using him as a way to become popular. The more Scott **pick**ed **on** David, the more the other kids liked Scott.

Mr. Lugano handed David a beaker★ full of some kind of **foul**-smelling chemical and asked him to fill six test tubes✶ halfway.

He heard several kids **snicker**.

Maybe his fly was down, he worried. No, he wouldn't look. What if he was standing in front of the room, this time facing the class, with his zipper down? Still he didn't look. If it was down, it was down. The damage was already done.

He heard more **laughter** as he continued to pour the chemical into the test tubes.

"What's that smell?" asked a girl from the front row.

"It smells like **rotten** eggs!" said someone else.

Maybe that was it. Maybe they were just laughing at the smell.

★ beaker 액체를 담는 실험용 기구.
✶ test tube 시험관. 기다란 원통형의 실험용 기구.

He tried to think about Carmelita. He thought about her whenever he was feeling **depress**ed. His problems were so **trivial compare**d to hers. And still, she was **laugh**ing **her head off.**

The image of Carmelita disappeared and instead he saw Mrs. Bayfield lying on her back in the rocking chair, her face covered with lemonade.

The beaker **slip**ped out of David's hand, fell on top of the test tubes, and the whole experiment **crash**ed to the floor.

The smell of rotten eggs **explode**d across the room like **tear gas.*** "Everyone outside!" ordered Mr. Lugano. "Now!"

The students hurried outside, **gag**ging, **cough**ing, but mostly laughing.

"Try not to breathe!" said Mr. Lugano.

David looked down. His pants were zipped. He ran out of the room with one hand over his nose and mouth.

Out on the **blacktop** Mr. Lugano explained what happened. He discussed the chemical reaction that had **taken place** and how the **molecule**s had been **dispersed** through the air to cause the **result**ing **odor.** It all made sense, logically and **scientific**ally.

But there was one thing that didn't make sense. Roger had broken Mrs. Bayfield's **pitcher** of lemonade. And now David had broken a pitcher. How do you explain that, Mr. Lugano?

"YOU KNOW, if someone else did it," said David a little later while eating lunch with Larry, "everyone would have thought

---

★ tear gas 최루가스. 눈물샘을 자극해서 눈물이 나오게 하는 독가스.

70

it was funny. Like if Roger Delbrook had done it, everybody would think it was real cool. He'd be **bragging** about it—'You hear about how I made a **stink bomb** in Lugano's class?' But because I did it, then it's not cool. It's, 'Did you hear what that stinkpot★ Ballinger did now?'"

"I know," Larry agreed. "It's just who you are. Roger or Scott could do anything they want, and it would be cool. But if you or I do the same thing, we're stinkpots."

They were sitting across from each other at the end of a long table. No one else was sitting at the table. That was partly because almost everyone else had finished their lunch, but it was also because Roger had walked past holding his nose and said loud enough for everyone to hear, "**Puke**, you stink!"

"You don't stink," said Larry. "I don't smell it on you."

"You sure?" asked David.

"I can't smell it at all," Larry **assured** him.

David looked at his ham and cheese sandwich, but he couldn't eat. The smell of rotten eggs was **stuck** in his throat. "I wonder what Carmelita is doing right now," he said.

"Yeah," Larry muttered, leaning on his elbows. "I **bet** she's doing okay," he said **hopefully**.

"Too bad she's not here," said David.

"Yeah," Larry agreed. "I wonder if she'd be my girlfriend or your girlfriend."

"Mine," said David with a laugh. Then more seriously he

★ stinkpot 악취를 풍기는 것.

said, "She wouldn't have to be the girlfriend of either of us. She could just be our friend. Besides, there's this other girl I kind of like."

"Really?" asked Larry. He sounded surprised, but then he said, "There's a girl I kind of like, too."

"Really?" asked David. He bit into his sandwich. He had to **concentrate** very hard to keep it from tasting like rotten eggs.

"What if Carmelita didn't like either of us?" asked Larry.

David looked at him, surprised, as he **swallow**ed his food. He had never thought of that.

"What if she thought we were **nerd**s?" asked Larry. "What if she came here and just turned into another Leslie Gilroy or Ginger Rice?"

"Carmelita's not like that," said David.

"How do you know?"

"She just doesn't seem that way."

"All you saw was a **naked** picture of her when she was nine years old."

"The way she was laughing," said David. "I bet Leslie Gilroy never laughed like that."

"Yeah," Larry agreed.

"Besides, she'd have to like us," said David, "if we're the ones who go down there and find her and **rescue** her and everything."

"I guess. But what if we weren't the ones who rescued her? Suppose she was born here, and never lived in Venezuela, and her parents had plenty of money. She might be Randy or Scott's

72

girlfriend."

David shook his head. "No way!"

"Maybe if Carmelita were born here," said Larry, "she wouldn't be able to laugh like that. Maybe it's not Leslie Gilroy's fault. It's just that all pretty girls in America **automatic**ally turn **snot**ty. There's nothing they can do about it."

"Maybe," David agreed, "except the girl I like is pretty, and she's not a snot."

"Yeah, the girl I like isn't a snot either," said Larry. "She's pretty, but not like Leslie or Ginger. I mean, I think a lot of kids think she's kind of strange."

"The kids think the girl I like is kind of **weird**, too," said David.

They looked at each other and the same thought **struck** them **simultaneous**ly. "I hope we don't like the same girl," said Larry.

David laughed. "So what, even if we do?" he asked. "It's not like she'll really want either of us to be her boyfriend!"

Larry smiled. "Yeah, I guess you're right," he said. "It's hard to imagine a girl like her ever liking a guy like me." He laughed. "It's hard to imagine any girl ever liking me." He shook his head. "I don't know. Maybe she would. Sometimes I think she does."

David thought about the way Miss Williams always said "Hello, Mr. Ballinger" or "Good morning, Mr. Ballinger" or "Good afternoon, Mr. Ballinger" whenever she saw him. If she didn't like him she wouldn't say that. Still, that didn't mean she wanted to be his girlfriend.

"So what's her name?" asked Larry.

"You tell me your girl's name."

"I asked you first."

David bit his lip. "I don't know her name," he admitted.

Larry laughed.

"I know her last name," said David. "Williams. There's this sort of game we play. Whenever we see each other we act very **proper** and **formal**. I say, 'Hello, Miss Williams,' and she says, 'Hello, Mr. Ballinger.'"

David waited for Larry's opinion on whether the game was stupid, or if it meant she liked him, but Larry **obvious**ly was thinking only about the girl he liked. "I don't know my girl's last name," he said.

"What does she look like?" asked David.

"Well, she's kind of little," Larry said, "**petite**. She has big brown eyes and real short brown hair."

"The girl I like has long red hair," said David.

Larry smiled. "Well, that's good anyway," he said.

"Does she know you like her?" asked David.

"No, I'm cool," said Larry. "She's in my math class. I stare at her all the time, but she can't tell where I'm looking 'cause of my **shade**s." Suddenly his **cheeks redden**ed. "That's her!"

David turned around. "Where?"

"Don't stare. She's heading toward the door to the library. She just walked past it. Don't let her know you're looking at her."

David tried to hide his eyes as he looked at the girl. He had to look twice to make sure he wasn't mistaken.

"Mo?" he asked. "She's in my shop class. I share a table with her."

"God, you're lucky!" said Larry. "Don't you think she's pretty? And she's really funny, too."

"Um, sure," said David. "I never really thought of her like that. I mean, being in shop, I guess because she's always hammering and **stuff** like that."

Larry **sigh**ed.

"Maybe if her hair wasn't so short—" David started to say.

"I like her hair like that," said Larry. "That's how girls wear their hair in France."

"How do you know?"

"I used to live there."

"I thought you lived in Venezuela."

"We moved to France after we left Venezuela," said Larry. "Mo **remind**s me of a girl I used to see every morning in a café in Paris."

15

DAVID WAS feeling pretty **crummy** as he headed home after school—until Miss Williams **pop**ped up. He was walking by the bike **rack**s and she was **bent** down **fiddling** with her bicycle lock, hidden by her bicycle. He didn't notice her until she suddenly popped up right next to him, as if out of a jack-in-the-box,★ and said, "Good day, Mr. Ballinger."

It **caught him** completely **off guard** and he didn't know what to do or say.

She smiled, glad to be the cause of his **befuddle**ment.

"Good day, Miss Williams," he said at last.

She **hop**ped on her bicycle and rode off.

He smiled as he watched her go, but he wondered what she thought about his **fiasco** in science class. She had to know about it. She probably even heard Roger say, "Puke, you **stink**!" to

---

★ **jack-in-the-box** 뚜껑을 열면 용수철에 달린 인형 등이 튀어나오는 장난감 상자.

him at lunch. And of course he didn't do anything about it. He just sat there.

As he headed home he tried to think of something else he could say to her the next time she popped up. He finally decided on "**Delightful** weather we're having."

He imagined the conversation. *Good afternoon, Miss Williams.*

Good afternoon, Mr. Ballinger.

Delightful weather we're having.

Yes, it is lovely, isn't it?

It wouldn't matter if rain was pouring down at the time. In fact, it would be funnier if it was.

He thought maybe he'd even wear a hat to school, so he could **tip** his hat when he spoke to her.

It was just so nice, **amid** all the garbage of junior high school, to be able to say "Hello, Miss Williams" to her and hear her say "Hello, Mr. Ballinger" to him. It was their own private joke,★ calling each other Miss Williams and Mr. Ballinger and speaking so **formal**ly. But besides being funny, there was also something very nice about it too.

He found himself thinking about her a lot over the weekend. He wasn't thinking anything in particular about her. She was just there, taking up all the space inside his head.

"It's your move," Ricky **remind**ed him.

"Huh?" asked David. "Oh," he said, looking at the chessboard.

He wondered if maybe he should try talking to her like a

★ private joke 특정 집단 내에서만 통하는 농담.

normal person. Maybe he could even ask her to go the school skate party with him next month?

"It's your move," said Ricky.

"Huh? Oh." He moved his bishop.★

Of course, just because she had said hello to him didn't mean she liked him enough to go to the skate party with him. He didn't even know her name.

She might not like him if he talked to her like a normal person. He couldn't **risk** that. He didn't want to chance **wreck**ing the only good thing in his life. At least he could still **daydream** about her; lying on the grass next to her, **count**ing her **freckle**s, laughing together, walking along a **desert**ed beach holding hands. He didn't want to lose his daydreams.

"Check," said Ricky.

And what about the **curse**? He didn't believe in curses, but still, how could he risk doing anything with her, when there was even a tiny chance that he might be cursed? What if he accidentally poured lemonade on her head?

It could happen very easily. They always **serve refreshment**s at skate parties. They probably had lemonade. And then she'd say, "I'm thirsty, Mr. Ballinger. Would you mind getting me a glass of lemonade?" So of course he'd have to get it, and he wasn't a very good skater to begin with, and the next thing he'd know he'd lose control, fall over her, and pour the lemonade on her face.

★ **bishop** 체스의 비숍. 대각선으로만 움직인다.

"Checkmate!" Ricky shouted **triumphant**ly.

David studied the board. He had nowhere to move his king.

"I can't believe it!" **exclaim**ed Ricky. "I **beat** you in chess!" He smiled **knowingly** at his brother. "You let me win, didn't you?"

"No," David **assured** him. "You beat me **fair and square**."

"I can't believe it! Wait till I tell Mom and Dad!"

David heard Ricky run through the house telling their parents how he beat David in a game of chess. He even told Elizabeth.

I'm the one who broke the window, thought David. *I* fell over in my chair. *I* forget to zip my fly. Mrs. Bayfield didn't do anything to me. I did it all to myself.

Somehow that didn't make him feel any better.

Well, there is one thing for certain, he decided. I am not, not, *not* going to pour lemonade on my head.

16

MO'S DOGHOUSE was finished. "I don't know how I'm going to get this stupid thing home," she complained.

David was leaning on his elbows, still feeling depressed after something that happened in homeroom. He glanced at Mo's huge project, with KILLER over the entrance.

He wanted to ask her why she built a doghouse if she didn't have a dog, but he was afraid she would take it the wrong way. "I'll help you carry it," he said.

She looked at him in surprise. "You?" she asked.

He didn't know if she was surprised that he would help her or because she thought he was a wimp and didn't think he could carry the heavy wooden doghouse.

"I could probably get a friend of mine to help, too," he said slyly. "Larry Clarksdale. Do you know him?"

She looked even more surprised. "Larry Clarksdale," she repeated. "Uh, yeah, I think I know who he is."

David tried to see if he could read anything into Mo's voice or the way she looked, but he couldn't. "He always wears blue sunglasses," he said.

Mo smiled.

Again David couldn't tell if she was smiling because she liked Larry or because she thought his sunglasses were **goofy**.

"So we'll meet you back here after school?" said David.

"Okay," said Mo.

"Me and Larry," said David.

"Okay," said Mo, staring **intent**ly at her project.

David smiled, glad to be able to help Larry. He looked at Mo and tried to imagine her sitting in a Paris café, but couldn't. Of course he had never seen a Paris café.

The reason he was depressed was because he had said "Good morning" to Miss Williams in homeroom, and she'd replied "Good morning, Mr. Ballinger," but she'd seemed **distract**ed, like she was thinking about something else and was in no **mood** to be **bother**ed. She'd seemed sad, too.

He didn't say "**Delightful** weather we're having." It suddenly seemed like a **dumb** thing to do.

He realized it was stupid to be depressed over something like that. She might have been tired, or maybe she had the Monday morning **blues**. Or something else could have been bothering her that probably didn't have anything to do with him. It could have been anything! She had a whole life that he knew nothing about. Who knows what could have been on her mind? Who knows what she did over the weekend?

It was just that saying hello to her and hearing her say "Hello, Mr. Ballinger" to him was the high point of his day. He had hoped it was a high point of her day, too, but maybe it didn't mean anything to her at all.

"**Puke**! What **stink**s?" said Randy, holding his nose. "Oh, it's David!"

Alvin laughed.

David tried to **ignore** them.

"Why don't you just go to another school?" asked Randy. "Why do you have to stink up this one?"

"**Lay off** him," said Mo. "He didn't do anything to you."

"He's the one who stunk up the whole school Friday," said Alvin. "I can still smell it!"

"I thought Randy **fart**ed," said Mo.

David laughed.

"What are you laughing at?" Randy **demand**ed.

David stopped laughing.

"He's laughing at you, fartface,★" said Mo.

Randy took a step toward Mo, but she held her ground and he backed off. "C'mon, Al," he said, leading Alvin away.

"You have to **stand up to** those assholes," Mo told David after they were gone.

"Yeah, well, it's easier for you," said David. "You're a girl."

"So?"

"So Randy wouldn't hit a girl."

★ fartface 방귀 뀔 때의 얼굴 표정이라는 뜻으로 못생겼다는 의미이다.

"Yeah, right," said Mo. "He's such a *gentleman*."

David smiled. He wished he had been the one who had called Randy fartface. *What are you laughing at?* asks Randy. *I'm laughing at you, fartface!* It would have been great. Except he knew he could never say anything like that. It wasn't only that he was afraid of Randy. He just couldn't imagine those words coming from his mouth.

At lunch he told Larry about how he had **arrang**ed for them to help Mo carry her doghouse home.

"Did she know who I was?" Larry asked.

David **nod**ded. "She remembered your blue sunglasses."

Larry smiled. "My **shade**s," he said, **tapp**ing his glasses just above the bridge of his nose. "Yeah, they're cool. So what else did she say? Did she say anything else about me?"

David repeated his **entire** conversation with Mo word for word.

Larry said "Hmmmm . . . ." several times as he listened very carefully.

David told him about Randy and Alvin and what Mo had said about farting.

"I told you she was funny," said Larry. "Besides being pretty, she has a great **personality**, too."

For the rest of the lunch **period** Larry switched back and forth, one moment very excited about his "date" with Mo, then the next being Joe Cool and acting like it was no **big deal**. Every once in a while he **giggl**ed. Finally, when lunch was almost over, he **abrupt**ly **declare**d, "I'm not going."

"What?" asked David.

"You should have asked me first, before just saying that I'd help," Larry pointed out. "How do you know that I don't have other plans?"

"What other plans?"

"I didn't say I had other plans. I said I could have had other plans. Maybe I had already promised to carry someone else's doghouse home."

"I **figure**d you'd want to walk home with Mo."

"Well, you figured wrong."

"What am I going to do now?" asked David. "It's too big for Mo and me to carry by ourselves."

"That's your problem," said Larry. "Oh, all right, I'll help you. But I'm not helping her. I'm helping *you*."

"Okay," said David.

"Okay," said Larry.

AFTER SPANISH they put their books away, then walked together to the shop room. Mo was sitting on top of a worktable, next to her doghouse.

"Hi," said David.

"Hi," she said. "Hi, Larry."

Larry **grunt**ed. He took his hands out of his pockets, **rub**bed them together, and said, "So where's this old doghouse?"

Mo looked at him like he was crazy.

"It's right there on the table," said David.

"Oh, yeah, right," said Larry. "Well, let's get to it."

Mo came down off the table. "Maybe you could see better if you took off your dark glasses," she suggested.

"Hey, I never take off my shades," said Larry.

The heaviest part of the doghouse was the back, since most of the front had been cut out to make a **doorway**. Larry and David took the back, and Mo, facing forward, held up the front as she led the way. Directly over her head was the word KILLER.

They just **barely** fit through the door.

They were halfway across the schoolyard when the **bark**ing started.

At first it was just Alvin and Randy.

Alvin had a high-pitched bark that sounded like "Arf-arf! Arf-arf!"

Randy's was more like "Grrr—ruff! Grrr—ruff!"

They were walking backward, barking in Mo's face.

David glanced at Larry, who looked back at him. He didn't know what else to do except hold up his corner of the doghouse and keep walking.

Roger and Scott joined in.

Scott howled, "Aaaaaoooooooo."

Roger said, "Woof, woof, woof!"

David could hear other kids around them laughing, and some of them barked once or twice too. He wondered if Miss Williams was among them.

"Hey, David, your pants are unzipped!" shouted Roger.

There was more **laughter**.

He was almost certain they were zipped. Besides, even if

they weren't, they were hidden by the doghouse.

"Grrr—ruff!"

"Arf-arf."

"Aaaaaoooo . . . ."

"Woof! Woof!"

Leslie and Ginger also barked but David thought they sounded more like sick cats.

"Don't get too close," **warn**ed Alvin. "She might bite you."

David felt the front of the doghouse **bang** to the ground. He looked around his corner to see Mo **chasing** Alvin.

"Mad dog! Mad dog!" Alvin **yell**ed as he easily **elud**ed her.

David remained by his corner of the doghouse. He didn't know what else to do.

Mo **trip**ped and fell in the grass.

Alvin stood over her barking while his friends laughed.

Mo picked herself up. "If I'm a dog," she said, "you know what you are? A bullock!★"

"Ooooh—a bullock!" Alvin said with a laugh. He smiled at his friends. "What's a bullock?"

Mo caught her breath. "It's a bull that's had its balls cut off."

Alvin's face turned bright red as Mo walked away, back toward the school building.

For a second David thought she was just going to leave him and Larry standing by her doghouse, but she turned around and headed back to them. She picked up her end of the doghouse and

---

★ bullock 수송아지.

86

said, "C'mon. Let's go."

He felt bad about not doing anything to help Mo, but what could he have done? Besides, Mo could take care of herself. Her last **remark** seemed to shut everyone up.

"Hey!" shouted Scott. "It's the Three Stooges!★ Mo, Larry, and *Curly!*"

That got everyone laughing again. "The Three Stooges," someone repeated.

"They even look like The Three Stooges!" said Roger.

"Except the real Three Stooges aren't as ugly," said Alvin.

David, Mo, and Larry carried the doghouse away. Roger and his friends didn't follow. David could hear them laughing about The Three Stooges. "Hey, Curly! Zip your fly!" called Scott.

What **rotten** luck, thought David. I would have to become friends with kids named Mo and Larry!

As he thought about it, he realized that Mo did sort of look like Moe from The Three Stooges. He smiled in spite of himself.

★ **The Three Stooges** 미국에서 1920년대부터 1970년대까지 큰 인기를 누린 코미디 팀. Moe, Larry, Curly의 3명의 멤버로 이루어져있다. 팀 이름의 'stooge'는 꼭두각시, 바보라는 뜻을 가지고 있다.

17

DAVID **HEAVED** a **sigh** of relief as they set the doghouse down in Mo's backyard. He **stretch**ed out his **stiff, cramp**ed arms.

Larry looked around nervously.

"You want something to drink?" Mo **offer**ed.

"Sure," said David.

Larry continued to look nervously around him.

Mo led them to the back door of her house. "You want water or something else?"

"Water's fine," said David.

"Larry?" asked Mo.

"Huh?" said Larry.

"Water?"

"Okay."

Mo reached behind a **bush** and turned on the hose. She took a drink from it, then handed it to David.

David took a long drink, then gave it to Larry. Larry's eyes **dart**ed back and forth as he drank.

"So where's Killer?" he finally asked.

"She doesn't have a dog," said David.

Larry relaxed.

Mo turned off the hose. "I want to get a dog," she explained, "but so far my parents won't let me. But once they see this **neat** doghouse, they have to let me get a dog, right? I mean, what good's a doghouse without a dog?"

"Right!" said Larry.

David was glad there was a **logical explanation**.

They walked back over to the doghouse. He and Larry sat on the grass and leaned against it. Mo lay on her back in front of them, looking up at the cloudy sky.

"Why do they hate me so much?" she asked. "It's not my fault I'm ugly."

David waited for Larry to say something, but Larry kept his mouth closed.

"You're not ugly," David finally said.

"Yeah, right," said Mo.

Again David looked at Larry, but he remained silent behind his blue sunglasses.

"It's me they hate," said David. "I used to be best friends with Scott—since the second grade—but he had to stop liking me in order to become popular. He has to prove to Roger and Randy that he's not my friend anymore. I guess he has to **make up for** all the years we were friends by hating me now."

"You were friends since the second grade?" asked Larry.

David nodded.

"I've never been friends with anybody for more than, I don't know, a couple of months. My family's always moving all the time. I've never even gone to the same school two years in a row."

"That must be tough," said Mo.

"I'm always the new kid," said Larry. "When I was little it wasn't so bad. It's easy to make friends when you're a little kid. You just find some other kid and go play. But now it seems like it's impossible to make new friends."

"I'm your friend," said David.

Mo laughed. "That's only because Scott started hating you," she said.

"That's not true," said David. "I'd be his friend anyway."

"What if Scott wanted to be your friend again?" asked Larry. "You'd probably start hating me, too, just so you could be popular like them."

"No, I wouldn't," David **insist**ed. "I wouldn't want to be one of them."

"I would," said Mo. "I don't care if Leslie and Ginger are the two biggest **pissant**s in the whole school. I'd trade places with them just like that"— she **snap**ped her fingers—"if I could be pretty like them."

David looked at Larry, but he kept his mouth shut.

"Nobody cares that they're pissants," Mo continued. "They're beautiful. That's all anyone cares about."

90

"You would never be a pi—like them." David **blush**ed.

"I would too!" said Mo. "If I was beautiful I'd be the most **revolting** pissant this world has ever seen."

David laughed.

"You're not ugly," Larry **blurt**ed out. "I mean, a lot of people probably think you're very attractive."

Mo made a sound like a horse. "Right," she said. "My grandmother!"

"No, really," said Larry. "In fact, there's this boy at our school—I can't say his name—but he told me he thinks you're beautiful."

"He's probably gay," said Mo.

Larry laughed.

"So what's your excuse, David?" asked Mo. "Larry's always moving and I'm ugly. How come you're one of The Three Stooges?"

"Oh, I don't know," said David. For a second he wasn't sure if he should tell them, but then he said very **matter-of-fact**ly, "There's a curse on me."

He waited for Larry or Mo to **react**, but they didn't.

"Okay, I don't know that I'm really cursed," he said. "But it sure seems that way."

"I know what you mean," said Mo. "Sometimes I think there's a curse on me, too. It's like no matter what I do, there's always something that **screw**s it **up**."

"Yeah, like when I go to a new school," said Larry. "I try real hard to be friendly and, you know, make a good **impression**, but something always happens. Like this year. It was my first day here, and some **idiot** isn't watching where he's going and **spill**s his chocolate milk in my **lap**. How am I supposed to make new friends and be cool and everything when I've got chocolate milk all over my pants? Who drinks chocolate milk anymore anyway?"

"I haven't had chocolate milk since I was a little kid," said Mo.

"That's what I mean," said Larry.

David decided not to try to explain his curse to them. He didn't think they'd believe him anyway. He didn't really believe it himself.

He figured he was probably no different than Larry or Mo or anyone else. Maybe everyone feels cursed.

"You guys don't know what a curse really is," said Mo. "At least you don't have **period**s! Now, that's a curse."

David and Larry blushed, then laughed to cover their **embarrass**ment.

Mo stood up and stretched, **obvious**ly proud of herself.

Larry and David also stood up. "You know, Mo," said Larry, "if you want your parents to let you have a dog, maybe you should change the name on your doghouse."

Mo looked at Larry, then at the doghouse, then back at Larry. She smiled at him.

18

THE FOLLOWING morning was cold, gray, and **miserable**. It wasn't raining, but there was a heavy **mist** in the air. Rain would have been an **improve**ment.

Miss Williams was wearing a shiny black plastic rain jacket. "Good morning, Mr. Ballinger," she said as David stepped away from his locker. Her green eyes **flash**ed at him.

"Good morning, Miss Williams," he **gallant**ly replied, glad that she seemed to like him again, after being so **distant** yesterday.

They walked **side by side** to Mr. MacFarland's class. Neither said a word, until finally, just before they reached the door, he decided to **take a chance**. "Delightful weather we're having."

As soon as he said it, he wished he hadn't. It was so stupid.

Miss Williams looked up at the gray and **gloomy** sky. She had a very **quirky** expression on her face. "Yes, quite," she answered.

They entered the classroom and headed to their **respective** desks.

Yes, quite, thought David. It was the perfect thing to say.

He couldn't stop thinking about her all morning, in homeroom, math, and on into **recess**. He **reliv**ed their conversation again and again.

Good morning, Mr. Ballinger. Good morning, Miss Williams. Delightful weather we're having. Yes, quite.

Yes, quite. It was perfect. She was perfect. Yes, quite perfect.

"David," said Larry.

"Huh?"

"Earth to David," said Mo. "Come in, please. Anybody there?"

"What?"

Larry and Mo laughed.

"He's probably thinking about his *girlfriend*," said Larry.

"Oooh, does David have a girlfriend?" asked Mo.

"Well, there's a girl he likes," said Larry. "Except he won't tell me her name."

David felt himself **redden**. He **glare**d at Larry. Didn't Larry realize how easily he could **turn the tables** on him? All he'd have to do was tell Mo that Larry was secretly in love with her. Or maybe—it suddenly **occur**red to him—Larry wanted him to do that.

"Oh, I **bet** I know who it is!" **declared** Mo. "Tori Williams! Am I right?"

Actually David didn't know if she was right or not, but he

94

figured she probably was. The last name was right.

"I've seen you and Tori making moon eyes★ at each other," said Mo.

Larry laughed.

Well, now he knew her name.

"At least she's not a **snot**," said Mo. "Although you have to admit she is a little **spacey**."

"Perfect for David," Larry said with a laugh.

Tori Williams, thought David as he headed to science. And Mo didn't just say she saw him making moon eyes at her. She said she saw *them* making moon eyes at *each other*. Tori Williams. It was a nice name. Yes, quite.

He saw Miss Williams, Tori, at lunch. He had just gotten out of shop and was on his way to his locker. She was angling across the grass in his direction. Her arms were **wrap**ped around her books, pressed against her chest. Her red hair hung on both sides of her shoulders.

She hadn't seen him yet. He wondered if he should call her Tori. He kind of hoped she wouldn't notice him. She was nice to him this morning and that was good enough. He didn't want to **press his luck**.

"Good afternoon, Mr. Ballinger," she said.

"Good afternoon"—he paused—"Miss Williams" He couldn't call her Tori.

She remained by his side as he continued to his locker. He

★ moon eyes 사랑에 빠진 눈빛.

glanced at her, and her green eyes flashed back at him. They both smiled. He wondered if this was what Mo would call "making moon eyes."

He stopped at this locker. "My locker," he told her. She stopped, too.

He turned the **combination**: 32 left, 16 right, 22 left. He pulled up on the handle but the locker didn't open. He tried it again, 32-16-22, but it still didn't open.

He smiled **sheepish**ly at Miss Williams. Tori. She **shrug**ged.

He wondered if it had anything to do with the **curse**. But how? What did they do to Mrs. Bayfield that had anything to do with a lock or a locker?

He was about to try again when he realized his mistake. He felt himself blush as he explained, "That was the combination to my gym locker."

"I do that sometimes, too," said Miss Williams. Tori.

David tried again, this time using the correct combination. The locker still wouldn't open. "What the . . . .?" he **mutter**ed.

Tori Williams bit her bottom lip and shrugged. She pushed out one side of her face with her tongue.

He looked back at the locker, then felt a **sink**ing feeling in the **pit** of his stomach. It was the wrong locker. His locker was the next one over. He didn't **dare** tell her that. "I don't know what's wrong," he said, stepping away from the locker. "I'll have to go talk to the **janitor**."

"You can put your books in my locker if you want," said Tori Williams.

96

"No, that's okay," said David. "I'll go talk to the janitor."

She looked around. "Well, so long, Mr. Ballinger."

"Bye, Miss Williams," he said. She started to walk away. "Tori."

She stopped. "David," she said without turning around, then continued on her way.

He made sure she was gone, then went to the right locker and opened it. He put his science book and notebook away and took out his lunch.

Then it hit him. Why *didn't* I put my books in her locker? That would have been perfect. Damn! That would have been great.

Yes, quite.

"HERE COMES Stooge number three!" announced Roger.

David could feel everyone turn and look at him as he made his way across the lunchroom to where Larry and Mo were sitting. He just hoped he wouldn't trip or something. Actually he did feel like a stooge for not putting his books in Tori's locker.

Neither Larry nor Mo said a word as he sat down across from them. Roger and his friends were at the next table.

"Hi, Curly," said Randy. "How ya doin'?"

David noticed that Ginger was wearing Scott's fringed leather jacket. That meant Scott was now going steady with one of the most popular girls in school.

And all he had to do was hate me, thought David. If only I

had put my books in Tori's locker. That would have been just as good as her wearing my jacket. Even better!

"I like your jacket, Ginger," said Mo. "It looks like it's made out of genuine *rat* skin."

David smiled. Mo could say anything to anybody.

Ginger **stared** at Mo.

"What's the matter, Ginger?" asked Mo. "Rat got your tongue?★"

Larry laughed.

"Gee, I'm sorry, Mo, but I can't talk to you," said Ginger. "I'm not allowed to talk to *boys*."

Mo turned bright red.

"That shut her up," said Leslie.

As soon as Roger and his friends left Larry **cracked up** laughing.

"What's so funny?" said Mo.

"She said she wasn't allowed to talk to you, but she had to talk to you to tell you that!"

"So?" demanded Mo.

"So she talked to you, when she said she couldn't."

"So?" asked Mo again.

Larry shrugged. "I don't know," he said.

"I know," said Mo. "You don't know anything."

She got up and walked away.

★ rat got your tongue? '말문이 막혔니?'라는 뜻의 'cat got your tongue?'이라는 표현에서 cat을 rat으로 바꾼 농담.

19

"WHAT DOES a cow say?" asked David.

Elizabeth **concentrate**d very hard. She pressed her lips together tightly and said, "Mmmmm."

"Moooo," said David.

"Mmmm," said Elizabeth.

David laughed. Then Elizabeth laughed too.

"Hi, Liz'beth," said Ricky, entering her room.

"Hi, Ricky!" said David, **exaggerating** the words to **encourage** his sister.

Elizabeth smiled.

"Hey, David, can I ask you something?" said Ricky.

"Sure."

"I was just wondering about something. We were talking about famous comedians today at school. Urn, who are The Three Stooges?"

David felt his stomach tighten. "The Three Stooges," he

said, trying to be as **matter-of-fact** as Ricky. "They're some old-time comedians. They were always hitting each other and breaking things and **stuff** like that."

He wondered what Ricky knew. Roger's brother, Glen Delbrook, was in Ricky's class.

"They kind of acted stupid?" asked Ricky. "**Goony**?"

"No. Well, maybe. It was more, just kind of, I don't know . . . . They were funny. It's a kind of humor known as slapstick comedy.★ They were very funny; very well respected in their field."

"Was one of them named **Curly**?" asked Ricky.

"Yes."

"Did he have real curly hair?"

"No," David suddenly realized. "He was **bald**. I guess that was the joke. They called him Curly even though he was bald. Why do you ask?"

"No reason," said Ricky. "We were just talking about comedians at school. Glen said his favorite comedian was Robin Williams,✶ and I said mine was Woody Allen.✳"

David knew that Ricky knew that David liked Woody Allen.

"And then some stupid girl said her favorite comedian was Curly of The Three Stooges."

"Oh," said David. "Well, he was funny, too. Very well

★ slapstick comedy 슬랩스틱. 과장되고 우스운 행위 등을 주요한 웃음거리를 사용하는 코미디.

✶ Robin Williams 로빈 윌리엄스. 미국의 배우이자 코미디언.

✳ Woody Allen 우디 앨런. 미국의 코미디언이자 영화감독.

respected in his field. I think The Three Stooges are on TV late at night. We could tape it and watch it tomorrow."

"No, that's okay," said Ricky. "I think I **get the idea**."

"So what do you want to do?" asked David. "Want to play chess or something?"

"Nah," said Ricky. "I got a lot of homework." He walked out of the room.

DAVID'S MOTHER was making chicken and dumplings★ for dinner. She asked David to put the **sack** of **flour** back on the shelf for her.

He stood on the **counter** and put the sack on the top shelf, jumped down, and landed hard on the linoleum⁑ floor. The sack of flour **tip**ped over and fell on his head.

Ricky **burst** out laughing.

It took David a few seconds to **figure out** what had happened. His curly hair had turned white with flour.

Even his mother laughed.

"Is that like something Curly of The Three Stooges would have done?" asked Ricky.

David smiled. "Yeah, I guess so," he said.

It wasn't until later that night, when David was lying in bed, that he realized the curse had **struck**—if there *was* a curse, and he didn't believe in curses.

Roger and Randy had **trampled** all over Mrs. Bayfield's

★ dumpling 밀가루와 계란을 끓는 스프나 스튜에 넣어서 익히는 요리.
⁑ linoleum 실내 바닥에 까는 재료.

flower garden. They had stepped on her flowers. Now the flour had "stepped" on him.

Oh, come on, now, he thought. That's really pushing it.★ Flowers and flour are completely different things. Just because they sound alike—that shouldn't mean anything.

All it proved was that if you really want to believe something, you can always find some way to make it seem true. Just like those stupid **horoscope**s.

Still, he had to admit it is pretty strange for a sack of flour to suddenly fall on your head. That kind of thing doesn't usually happen.

He thought about talking to his dad about his problems—telling him about what they'd done to Mrs. Bayfield, and then about all the things that had happened to him. Maybe his dad would be able to find some kind of **logical, scientific explanation** for everything.

Except he was too **ashamed** to tell his father that he helped steal a **cane** from a poor old lady. And he would be too **embarrass**ed to talk about all the things that had happened to him. His dad probably would just tell him to go **apologize** to her.

Besides, what kind of scientific explanation could there possibly be? No, science had nothing to do with it. There were only two possible explanations. Either he was cursed or he was a stooge. It was **one or the other.**

★ **push it** 너무 극단적으로 생각하다.

20

HE DECIDED to tell his friends about the curse. "Do you know Felicia Bayfield?" he asked on Friday at recess.

"Who?" asked Larry.

"I know her," said Mo. "She's this old, **spacey** lady who wears a lot of funny clothes."

"Sounds like Tori Williams," said Larry. He and Mo laughed.

"She's a **witch**," said David. "She **murder**ed her husband. She removed his face."

"Ugh!" said Mo.

"He lived for a while," said David, "but you can't live too long without a face. But his face is still alive. It's hanging on a wall of her house. She put it in some kind of special **solution** to **preserve** it. And she talks to it, and it talks back."

David didn't like saying mean things about Mrs. Bayfield, but he had to **convince** his friends she was really a witch. Little did he know that one day his own face would be hanging on the wall of her house.

"I wonder what a person would look like without a face," said Larry. He thought a moment. "Wouldn't there just be another face behind it? How thick is a face?"

"Real thin," said Mo. "Thinner than paper. And behind it you just have **blank** skin that you could almost see through, with holes where the eyes, nose, and mouth used to be."

"Like a ghost," said Larry. "Except you're alive."

"A Doppelgänger," said David.

"What?" asked Mo.

"I don't know," said David, shaking his head. "Remember when I said I thought I was cursed?" he asked. "Well, it wasn't like you thought. Mrs. Bayfield put a curse on me. She said my Doppelgänger will **regurgitate** on my soul."

He started at the beginning. He told them about how he had helped Roger, Scott, and Randy steal her snake-head cane, except he made it sound like he was the one who led the attack.

". . . Then she said in a really **creepy** voice, 'Would you boys like some lemonade?' Except I don't think it was really even lemonade."

"What'd you do?" asked Larry.

"You didn't drink it, did you?" asked Mo.

"No. As I was pouring it in my glass I **pretend**ed to trip, then I **knock**ed her rocking chair over and poured the lemonade right on her face!"

"All right!" cheered Mo.

He didn't want to tell them that he really just stood around while the other boys knocked her over in her chair and poured lemonade on her head. It wouldn't make sense. Why would she put a curse on him if he had just stood there while everyone else did everything?

"I **toss**ed the empty **pitcher** away," he said, "but it accidentally went into her window. It broke the window and the pitcher."

The more he lied, the more he got into it. But at the same time he felt a **horrible** sense of **guilt** right in the **pit** of his stomach. It only **bother**ed him a little at first, but the feeling grew, like Pinocchio's★ nose, with each lie.

"Roger, Randy, and Scott ran away with her cane, but I stood over her. Her legs were up in the air. If you think her clothes are **weird**, you should see her **underpants!**"

"You saw her underpants!" **exclaim**ed Larry.

"What'd they look like?" asked Mo.

"It was like they were made out of spider webs," said David. "And there were spiders **crawl**ing all around and some other kinds of bugs, too."

"**Gross**," said Mo.

"So then I **flipp**ed her **off**," said David. "You know, **gave** her **the bird**."

"Good going," said Mo.

"That's when she said the thing about my Doppelgänger."

"What's a Doppelgänger?" asked Larry.

"I looked it up in the dictionary. It means the **ghostly**

★ Pinocchio 피노키오. C. 콜로디의 동화에 등장하는 나무 인형으로, 거짓말을 하면 코가 길어진다.

counterpart of a living person."

"What's that?" asked Mo.

"I don't know." He explained the curse to them, but he **exaggerate**d that, too.

". . . And I was playing catch with my little brother and I threw the ball right to him, but it suddenly curved in **midair** and **crash**ed into my parents' bedroom window."

Larry and Mo were **skeptical** at first, but as David went over each **incident** they had to admit that if nothing else, it was a lot of weird **coincidence**s.

"Are you sure you're not making this up?" asked Mo.

"You know about the beaker I broke in science class," David **remind**ed her. "And Larry, remember what happened to me in Spanish?"

"That's right!" Larry exclaimed.

"Oh, yeah, I heard about that," said Mo. "Your **fly** was down and you didn't know it."

David **blush**ed. "It was because I saw her underpants," he explained. "Everything I did to her has happened to me. Except so far I haven't poured lemonade on my head. That's probably next. Oh, and I also flipped off my mother."

"You flipped off your mother!" exclaimed Mo.

David shrugged.

"I don't believe it," said Mo. "You wouldn't flip off your own mother!"

"I was just waving to her," he explained, "when suddenly I got like a **cramp** in my hand, and all my fingers **bent** down except the middle one."

"No!" said Mo.

"It was really no **big deal**," said David. "It was just a cramp. Besides, it's not such a bad thing to do, when you think about it. Why is raising your middle finger any worse than raising any other finger?"

"It just is," said Mo. "It's the most horrible thing you can do!"

"Why?" asked David. "Most people probably don't know what it means." He turned to Larry. "You've lived in other countries. Do they know what it means there?"

"They do it differently in different countries," Larry explained. "In Spain they do it like *this!* In Hong Kong they do it like *this!*" He **demonstrate**d the **gesture** for each country. "In Italy they do it like *this!*"

Mr. Lugano **happen**ed **by** at that moment. He **grab**bed Larry's shoulder and said, "You're coming with me, young man!"

Mr. Lugano was Italian.

21

DAVID DIDN'T see Larry again until Spanish class. "What did Mr. Lugano say to you?" he asked after class was over. "Did you get in trouble?"

Larry smiled. "He couldn't do anything! First he was going to send a note home to my parents telling them what I did, except he couldn't figure out how to write it in a note. So then he told me I had to tell my parents what I did. But then I said, 'What did I do?' And he said, 'You know.' And I said, 'No, I don't.' So finally he just told me not to do it again, and I said, 'Do what?'"

David laughed, but **abrupt**ly stopped when he saw Scott, Randy, and Roger coming.

Scott, Randy, and Roger were walking down the center of the **sidewalk** next to the row of outside lockers. There wasn't room for David and Larry to get by.

David stepped aside to let them pass.

Roger **glance**d at David, then turned to Scott and said loud enough for everyone to hear, "Hey, Scott, are you going out with Ginger again on Saturday night?"

"Sure," said Scott, **equal**ly as loud. "You and Leslie want to join us?"

"Hey, that sounds like a good time," said Roger.

"How about you, Randy?" Scott asked. "Why don't you and Tori join us?" He said the name Tori especially loud.

"Yeah, that Tori Williams is one hot babe!" said Roger.

"Maybe I will," said Randy.

David's face burned, even though he was fairly sure they had said all that just **for his benefit**. Somehow Scott must have found out that he liked Tori Williams. Maybe Scott also saw them making moon eyes at each other.

But Randy still might ask her out for Saturday night, he realized, just because Randy knew David liked her. He wondered if Tori would agree to go out with Randy. She must know Randy's a **jerk**. But then he remembered that he himself once thought Randy was a good guy. Randy was good at pretending he wasn't a jerk.

"You shouldn't have stepped out of their way," said Larry.

"Huh?"

"You lost face," said Larry.

"What are you talking about?"

"It's a Japanese expression," said Larry. "You reminded me of it when you were talking about Mrs. Bayfield stealing people's faces. I used to live in Japan, you know."

"No, I didn't know. I don't even know what you're talking about."

"You know how Mo always tells you to stand up for yourself. It's the same thing. When you don't stand up for yourself, the Japanese say you lose face. Like just now, when those guys were coming toward us. We have just as much right to walk on the sidewalk as they do. You stepped aside, so you lost a little face."

"There wasn't room for all of us," said David. "What was I supposed to do? Push my way through them? It's not worth getting in a fight over."

"Every time they **push you around** and you do nothing about it, you lose a little more of your face," said Larry.

David **rub**bed his face with his hand. "They push you around too," he said. "I don't see you doing anything about it."

"That's different."

"How?"

"I don't have to fight. I know kung fu."

"Yeah, right," said David.

"I do," said Larry. "I have a black belt. If I had to, I could take on all three of them at once." He karate-**chop**ped the air in front of him. "They wouldn't have a chance."

"Yeah, right," said David.

"But that's not *the way* of kung fu," Larry continued. "It's always best to walk away from a fight. Like remember when they wouldn't let me use the bathroom? I just walked away. You only fight if you have no other choice. Sometimes it takes more courage to walk away than it does to fight."

"Well, how come it's all right for you to walk away, but if I walk away I lose part of my face?"

Larry didn't answer. "You know what you should do," he said. "You should call up Tori Williams and ask her out for Saturday night, before Randy."

"Randy's not going to ask her out," said David. "They were just saying that. Besides, you know I can't ask her out."

"Why not?"

"There's a **curse** on me, remember? What if I take her to a movie and then pour lemonade on my head. Or her head?"

"That's not going to happen," said Larry. He **shrug**ged. "Just don't drink any lemonade."

"What if she asks me to get her a cup of lemonade?"

"Tell her they don't have any. Get her a Coke★ or something."

"You don't realize how powerful the curse is. Even if I ordered a Coke, the person behind the counter would probably make a mistake and give me a lemonade. Then as I'm about to hand it to Tori, there'd be an **earthquake** or something, and I'd trip and pour it right on her head! No, there's no way I can take her out so long as I'm cursed."

"Yeah, right," said Larry.

David **force**d a laugh.

"What?" asked Larry.

"Oh, I was just thinking," said David. "Those guys all think

★ Coke 코카콜라.

they're so tough. They have no idea you know kung fu. They don't know you could **tear** them apart."

"Right," said Larry. "But only if I couldn't walk away." He smiled. "Too bad about the curse. Otherwise you and Tori would have a great time together."

They had reached an understanding. If David would believe Larry knew kung fu, Larry would believe that the only reason David didn't ask Tori Williams out on a date was because of the curse.

"Hey, Larry," said Mo, coming up behind them. "Will you teach me that?"

"What?"

"You know, how to give someone the finger in Italian."

22

FRIDAY AFTERNOON and evening David couldn't stop thinking about Tori—and Randy. What if he really did ask her out? What would she say to him? *She might be talking on the phone to him right now.*

Saturday he worried about their date. He wondered where they went, what movie they saw. Was it **rated** R?★ What else did they do? Did he put his arm around her? *He might be kissing her right now.*

Sunday he wondered if she was in love with him. What if she came to school wearing Randy's jacket? She wouldn't be allowed to talk to him anymore, not even "Hello, Mr. Ballinger."

He was glad he hadn't put his books in her locker. He'd never be able to get them out. Maybe she's been in love with

★ R-rate 보호자 없이는 청소년은 볼 수 없는 영화 등급.

Randy all along. Maybe she was just pretending to be nice to David, like Randy used to do. It was some kind of big joke. She pretended to like David, but really she and her friends were all laughing at **Curly**, the stooge.

Monday morning he was standing outside the door to Mr. MacFarland's class when he saw her coming toward him. He didn't know whether to say hi to her anymore. At least she wasn't wearing Randy's jacket. She had on a long multicolored kind of **shawl**.

"Hi," he said.

She was still a couple of yards★ away, and he said it so quietly he didn't think she even heard him.

"Hi, David," she said. Her green eyes **flash**ed as she **breezed** into the room.

"Hi," he said again, in case she didn't hear him the first time. Feeling like a total fool, he **eased** his way through the desks to his seat.

Actually, he realized, whether or not he was a fool depended on whether or not she heard the first hi. If she did, then he was a fool for saying hi twice. She and Randy would probably have a good laugh over it together.

On the other hand, if she didn't hear him say the first hi, then that meant she thought she said the first hi. That'd be good. If you say the first hi to someone it means you're making an **effort** to be nice to that person, but if you say the second hi

---

★ yard 길이의 단위 야드. 1야드는 0.9144미터이다.

then maybe you're just being polite.

Big deal! he **chide**d himself. Who cares who said the first hi? He closed his eyes. Big deal. I don't care. I don't care. I don't . . .

He looked at Tori. She seemed half asleep as she **thumb**ed through the pages of her social studies book. Little did she know what a simple hi had done to him.

I have no face, he thought.

He had thought about what Larry had said about losing face. If I had a face, he thought, I would just go up to Tori Williams and talk to her and tell her how I feel. If I had a face, I wouldn't let Roger and his friends push me around. I would never have laughed at all their stupid jokes.

I would never have gone with them to steal Mrs. Bayfield's **cane**. I would have stood up for her and told them to leave her alone. I would have told her I was sorry instead of giving her the finger. I have a finger, but I don't have a face.

Maybe my Doppelgänger is wearing my face.

He realized that what he should do was go back to Mrs. Bayfield's house and tell her he was sorry. **Better late than never.** If she had put a curse on him, that'd be the only way she'd remove it. But even if there was no curse, he should still tell her he was sorry. It was the right thing to do.

He knew what he should do, but he also knew he wouldn't do it. Because he had no face.

"WE **FIGURED** it **out**!" Mo told him at **recess**. "We know how to remove your curse! Larry figured it out."

Larry smiled. "It was so simple, I don't know why I didn't think of it sooner."

"I know," David **mutter**ed. "Tell Mrs. Bayfield I'm sorry."

"Huh?" said Larry. "No. That wouldn't work. No, I got it all figured out."

"He does," Mo agreed. "It's perfect."

"What?" asked David.

"You have to pour a pitcher of lemonade on your head," said Larry. He smiled, proud behind his blue sunglasses.

"Are you crazy?" asked David.

"Mrs. Bayfield put a boomerang★ curse on you," Larry explained. "They're actually pretty common in Australia."

"Larry lived in Australia for six months," said Mo.

Somehow, David wasn't surprised.

"Everything you did to Mrs. Bayfield has happened to you, right?" Larry asked him. "It's the classic Australian boomerang curse. Except you haven't poured a pitcher of lemonade on your head. Once you do that, the boomerang will have **gone full circle** and the curse will be over."

"No way!" David **protest**ed. "I'm not pouring lemonade on my head."

"Look, it's going to happen anyway," said Larry. "At least this way it will be under controlled conditions. You'll be at home with me and Mo. Would you rather it happened

---

★ **boomerang** 부메랑. 던지면 목표물을 치고 되돌아오는 가운데가 굽은 나뭇조각. 여기에서는 무엇인가가 되돌아온다는 의미로 쓰였다.

unexpectedly? Here at school? Or in front of Tori?"

"He's right," said Mo.

"I don't *know* that it's going to happen anyway," said David. "Maybe the curse is already over."

"Good, then ask Tori out on a date," said Larry.

"I can't. The curse may be over and it may not. I just don't know. I may never know. Besides, I think she already went out with Randy on Saturday."

"So you can ask her out for next Saturday," said Larry.

"I don't think you're afraid of the curse," said Mo. "I think you're afraid of Tori."

"I'm not afraid of—"

"Then **dump** a pitcher of lemonade on your head," said Mo.

"It's the only way," said Larry.

"Then you can go out with Tori," said Mo. "Unless you're chicken.★"

AFTER SCHOOL, MO and Larry walked home with David to watch him dump lemonade on his head.

"Why do you have to watch?" David asked. "Why can't I just do it by myself?"

"There always have to be **witness**es," said Larry.

David thought it was **ridiculous**. He really didn't believe he was cursed, but even if he was, there was no **guarantee** that this would **cure** him. *A boomerang curse!* **Give me a break.** Where

---

★ chicken '닭'이 아니라 '겁쟁이'라는 의미로 쓰였다.

does Larry come up with these things?

He opened the door of the **freezer** and removed a can of frozen lemonade **concentrate**. "It's not going to work," he said. "It's pink lemonade."

"So?" asked Mo.

"So, Mrs. Bayfield's lemonade wasn't pink."

"Will that make a difference?" Mo asked Larry, *the expert*.

Larry rubbed his **chin**. "It doesn't matter," he **declared**. "As long as it's lemonade."

David looked at him in **disbelief**. He **peel**ed off the top of the can and dumped the **contents** into the **blender**. Then he added four cups of water. He **stared** at the pink turd★ in the bottom of the blender.

"Turn it on," said Mo.

"What if you're both part of the curse?" he asked.

"What do you mean?" asked Larry.

"Maybe somehow Mrs. Bayfield got into your heads and made you **convince** me to dump a pitcher of lemonade on my head."

"She didn't get into my head," said Larry. "I'd know it if she got into my head. At least I think I would."

"It's just that there is no other way I would have poured lemonade on my head," said David.

"You don't know that," said Larry.

"Everything that has happened to me I've done to myself,"

★ turd 똥 같은 것.

said David. "*I* broke my parents bedroom window. *I* flipped off my mother. *I* forgot to zip my fly. *I* dropped the beaker in science class. *I* leaned too far back in my chair and fell over. But there is no way I would ever have poured lemonade on my head."

"A curse is a curse," said Mo.

"You'd pour it on yourself anyway," said Larry.

"At least now it's in a controlled **circumstance**. It's like when a **bomb squad** blows up a bomb. The bomb's going to **explode** anyway, but at least they make sure no one gets hurt by it."

David pushed the button on the blender. Very quickly he had a pitcher full of **foam**y pink lemonade. They took it outside to the backyard.

"I never used to be friends with you," David pointed out. "We didn't become friends until after Mrs. Bayfield put the curse on me."

"So what's that supposed to mean?" asked Mo.

"Maybe Mrs. Bayfield made me be friends with you. Maybe she knew Larry used to live in Australia. Maybe she knew you'd make me pour lemonade on my head."

"Look, do you want to go out with Tori or don't you?" Mo demanded.

"Sure I want to go out with her," said David.

"Well, then shut up and dump it on your head!"

David took off his shirt and sat down on the grass. He held the pitcher of lemonade at shoulder level. "This is so stupid," he told them. Holding the pitcher **steady**, he lay down flat on his back.

"Go ahead," said Mo.

He held his breath, then **tip**ped the pitcher, slowly at first. A couple of drops **splatter**ed on his **forehead**. He quickly tipped it the rest of the way, dumping the whole thing on his face.

Larry and Mo **crack**ed **up**.

David sat back up and waited for them to stop laughing.

"So how do you feel?" asked Larry.

"Like a jerk," said David. "A **sticky**, wet jerk."

They laughed again.

David had taken off his shirt so it wouldn't get wet, but now he picked it up and used it to wipe his face.

"Well, what about the curse?" asked Mo. "Is it gone?"

David stood up. "I don't know," he said. "Maybe I do feel a little lighter. Like I'd been carrying around a heavy weight and it's no longer there."

"That's the curse," said Larry.

"Go call Tori," said Mo.

"Not yet," said David. "I have to be certain the curse is really gone. I'll wait a month, and if there's absolutely no sign of the curse, then I'll call her."

"A month!" exclaimed Mo.

"Three weeks," said David.

"One day," said Mo. "That's all!"

"I have to be sure the curse is really gone."

"Three days," said Larry. "That's the standard waiting **period** in Australia. You'll still be able to ask her out for Saturday night." He checked his watch. "It is now four seventeen, Monday. If the curse doesn't **strike** by four seventeen on Thursday, then you have to call Tori."

23

LARRY AND MO went home. David brought the **blender** and his wet shirt back into the house.

Ricky was sitting at the kitchen **counter**. His face was **buried** in his arms, which were folded on top of the counter.

"Hey, Rick," said David. "Are you all right?"

He didn't answer.

David set the blender **pitcher** in the **sink**, then walked over to his brother. "What's the matter?" he asked, putting his hand on Ricky's shoulder.

Ricky **jerk**ed his shoulder free as he looked up at David. His eyes were red and **swollen** as if he'd been crying, and his face was dirty and **bruise**d. He quickly stood up and headed into the hall.

"Ricky?" said David as he started to follow.

"Go away!" Ricky **yell**ed. "I hate you!" He disappeared into his room.

David returned to the kitchen and washed the pitcher. Whatever it was, he thought, Ricky will get over it. He had a feeling it might have something to do with Ricky finding out he was one of The Three Stooges.

Well, I never told Ricky I was someone great. He's the one who **built me up** so much. He had to find out the truth **sooner or later**. It's not my fault.

The glass pitcher **slip**ped out of his hand and fell to the floor. He looked at it in horror.

It wasn't broken.

He shook his head. That was close, he thought. If the pitcher had broken, it would have meant the curse was back and he wouldn't be able to ask Tori out on a date.

He tried to decide if he really believed that Mrs. Bayfield had put a curse on him. Probably not. But if she did put a curse on him, did he really **get rid of** it by dumping lemonade on his head? Probably not. But if he did get rid of the curse, and nothing bad happened by Thursday afternoon, would he really have the courage to ask Tori Williams on a date? Probably not. But if he did ask her out, would she go with him? Probably not.

HE SAW Tori the next morning as he entered Mr. MacFarland's class. "Good morning, Mr. David," she said, smiling.

He turned away and **pretend**ed he hadn't heard her as he made his way to his desk. There was no point in trying to talk to her now. If the curse didn't strike by four seventeen on Thursday, he'd call her up and ask her out. There was no sense in **complicating** things by talking to her. She probably liked Randy anyway.

He leaned way back in his chair, balancing on the two back legs.

"SO, ANYTHING bad happen to you yet?" Larry asked at recess.

David shrugged. "My brother hates me." He was sitting on the grass, **squint**ing into the sun.

"Is that part of the curse?" asked Mo.

"No," David admitted. "I don't think so. I didn't do anything to Mrs. Bayfield that would cause her brother to hate her."

"My sister hates me," said Larry, "and I'm not cursed."

"I hate my brother," said Mo.

THE CURSE still hadn't struck by seven P.M. Tuesday, at least as far as David could tell. Maybe it struck and I don't even know it, he worried.

He was lying on the **couch** in the **den**, watching television.

"*This is Jim Rockford. At the tone leave your name and message. I'll get back to you.*"

Ricky walked into the room. For a moment he just stood in front of David, **block**ing his view. Then he picked up the remote control and changed the channel to wrestling.

David didn't say a word. He knew Ricky liked **rerun**s of *The Rockford Files* as much as he did, and that they both thought wrestling was stupid.

124

Taking the remote-control **device** with him, Ricky sat down in the chair and put his feet on the ottoman.★

"You want to play cards or something?" asked David.

Ricky stared at the TV. "Oooh, **neat**!" he **exclaim**ed as one of the wrestlers **slam**med the other to the canvas. "Aw-right!"

"You know you think that's stupid," said David.

"No, I don't!" **snap**ped Ricky. "Just because you think it's stupid doesn't mean I have to think it's stupid. I don't have to like everything you like. I think *Rockford's* stupid!" He looked back at the TV. One wrestler was stepping on the other wrestler's face while twisting his leg at the same time.

"Oh, wow, **radical**!" Ricky exclaimed.

David got up and started out of the room.

"You're the one who's stupid!" Ricky called after him.

WEDNESDAY MORNING David leaned back in his chair, balancing on the two back legs as he stared at the side of Tori's face. You don't know it, he thought, but if nothing happens today or tomorrow, I'm going to ask you out on a date. His stomach **churn**ed.

He tried to imagine the conversation.

She'd answer the phone. *Hello?*

Good evening, Miss Williams. This is Mr. Ballinger.

Good evening, Mr. Ballinger.

He decided it would be easier to ask her out if he called her

---

★ottoman 발걸이로 쓰이는 등받이 없는 쿠션 의자.

Miss Williams. Maybe he could ask her to tea.

I say, Miss Williams, would you care to have a spot of tea with me?

*I'd be **delighted**, Mr. Ballinger.*

"Mr. Ballinger!" said Mr. MacFarland.

David's chair **bounce**d forward as he sat up straight. "Yes."

"Does everyone have the right to be happy?"

David had no idea what Mr. MacFarland was talking about, but he could guess the answer from the way that Mr. MacFarland asked the question. "No," he said.

"That's correct," said Mr. MacFarland. "The Declaration of **Independence** says everyone has the right of the pursuit of happiness. What's the difference between the right to be happy and the right to **pursue** happiness?"

"Okay, um," said David, trying to fake it. "Not everyone's going to be happy all the time. I guess most people are **hardly** ever happy. You probably have to be sad sometimes in order to be happy. Sometimes you might think you want something, but then when you get it, it doesn't make you happy. You might be happier pursuing it than you are when you actually get it."

He had no idea if what he said **made sense** or not.

"Mr. Umbridge," said Mr. MacFarland. "Does that mean you have the right to do anything you want in order to pursue happiness? If smoking marijuana makes you happy, do you have the right to smoke marijuana?★"

★ marijuana 대마초.

126

"No."

"Why not?"

"Because it's supposed to be bad for you."

"Is that something the government should decide? Or should people be allowed to make their own choices? **Cigarette**s are bad for you, but they're not **illegal**. Alcohol is bad for you. Even television is bad for you. What if it was discovered that television caused **severe** brain damage? Should the government be allowed to make it against the law to watch television? Miss Peters."

"I don't think they could ever make television illegal. It's just like cigarettes. The cigarette companies are too powerful. Too many people would lose their jobs and . . . ."

When the bell rang, David quickly left his seat and hurried out the door so that Tori Williams wouldn't try to say good morning to him.

"YOU WANT to go with us to the park after school today?" Mo asked David at lunch. "We're going to watch **criminal**s pick up **trash**."

"See, every Wednesday criminals come to the park and pick up trash," Larry explained.

"**Robber**s and **murder**ers," said Mo.

"Well, I don't know if there are any murderers," said Larry. "I think they are mostly drunk drivers★ and **shoplift**ers."

★ drunk driver 음주 운전자.

"Oh, I thought there'd be murderers," said Mo, **obvious**ly disappointed.

"Well, maybe there are a few murderers," said Larry.

David figured Larry didn't want him along. "Sorry," he said. "I can't make it. Besides, I don't think I should be around murderers when I still might be cursed."

"The curse is gone," said Larry. "The lemonade took care of that."

"I just want to be careful," said David. "You said three days was the standard waiting **period**."

"You just want to be cursed so you don't have to ask Tori out on a date," said Mo.

"Bullshit," said David.

Larry and Mo looked **odd**ly at him. For some reason it sounded strange to hear David say "Bullshit."

He felt odd about it too, and **blush**ed right after he said it.

AFTER LUNCH he headed toward P.E.

"Hello, Mr. Ballinger," said Tori, hurrying alongside him.

"Hi," he muttered, looking down at the ground.

"I liked what you said in homeroom," she said, "about happiness. Having to be sad in order to be happy."

"Yeah, well, I just had to say something," he said, then walked quickly away from her and into the boys' locker room.

"Bye, David," he heard her say behind him.

He walked down the row of lockers. Lately he had begun to **dread** gym. He felt very **vulnerable** there, especially when

128

changing clothes. So far he'd been left pretty much alone, except for being called a few names. But he was **constant**ly afraid that Roger and some of his friends might try to steal his clothes or put a jockstrap★ over his face.

He tried not to run around too much during soccer. He didn't want to **sweat** too much because he didn't want to have to shower. When he returned to the locker room, he quickly changed his clothes, then went to the bathroom and **splash**ed his face with cold water.

"Your brother's got more **gut**s than you do," said Roger Delbrook. He was **comb**ing his hair in front of the bathroom mirror. "Sure Glen beat him up, but at least he fought back. That's more than you ever do. You just stand there like a pile of—"

The gym teacher entered the bathroom.

David headed outside. He saw Tori Williams coming out of the girls' locker room. He quickly turned before she **spot**ted him.

"WHAT'S WITH you and Ricky?" asked his mother. "He said he hated you."

"I don't know," said David. He was sitting at his desk doing his homework.

"I think you should go talk to him."

"I'm doing my homework," said David.

★ jockstrap 남자들이 운동 경기 때 차는 국부 보호대.

He wondered if Glen had really **beat**en up Ricky, like Roger had said. Was that why Ricky hated him?

He went into his closet, got his baseball and glove, then headed for his brother's room. He was surprised by how nervous he felt. "So, you want to play catch?" he asked.

Ricky didn't look up from his paperback book.

David stood in Ricky's room, **pound**ing the ball into his glove.

Ricky put his book down. "What do you want?"

"Did you get in a fight with Glen Delbrook?"

"What do you care?"

"I care. I'm your brother."

"Unfortunately!"

"What did I do?" asked David. "Just tell me what I did!"

"You're a stooge!" said Ricky.

"Look, just because Roger calls me names. That's his problem. Names don't hurt me."

"But it's true!" said Ricky. "You are a stooge. I saw you and your stoogy friends. You dumped a whole pitcher of pink lemonade on your head."

"Look, I—"

"Why'd you do that?" Ricky demanded. "If you're not a stooge, why'd you do that?"

David didn't know what to say. How could he tell Ricky about the curse? Ricky would only think he was a bigger fool. Ricky was too smart to believe in curses.

"Stooge!" said Ricky.

David walked out to the backyard. He **toss**ed the ball onto the **roof** of the house, then caught it when it rolled down. He tossed it up again. It **momentarily** disappeared from view, then he **lunge**d and caught it as it rolled off the roof.

"Careful," his mother called to him from the kitchen. "You already broke one window."

"I won't," said David.

He tossed the ball back onto the roof, just above the window.

24

THURSDAY.

David was wearing socks, no shoes. "I made orange juice," he said, holding the pitcher in his hand. "Anybody want some?"

"That's very nice, thank you," said his mother.

David poured a glass for his mother, holding the glass in one hand and the pitcher in the other. His feet **slid** a little bit as he handed it to her.

"Dad?" he asked.

"Sure," said his father. "Careful, not too full."

He didn't **spill** a drop.

"Hey, Ricky, you want some orange juice?" he asked as his brother entered the kitchen.

"I'm not thirsty," said Ricky.

David put down the pitcher.

Ricky walked over, picked up the pitcher, and poured himself a glass of orange juice.

HE SAW Tori Williams when he got to school. He didn't say anything to her, and this time she didn't try to say anything to him either. She just walked right past him as if he wasn't even there.

"I don't think she likes me," he told his friends at recess.

"You're just too chicken to ask her out," said Mo.

"No, I'm not. It's just that she **ignore**s me all the time. She won't even say hello to me anymore. I think she likes Randy."

"Well, you still have to call her up today," said Mo.

"Unless the **curse** strikes," said David. "I still have until four seventeen."

"You sound like you want the curse to strike," said Larry.

"No, I don't," David **insist**ed. "I just want to be sure it's gone, that's all."

"He's afraid to call up Tori," said Mo.

David changed the subject. "So," he asked, "did you go watch the **criminal**s pick up **trash**?"

"Yes!" exclaimed Mo. "They were so **scary**. You should have been there. There were **robber**s and **murder**ers. You could tell they were planning an escape, too."

"A criminal spoke to her," said Larry.

"It was **horrible**!" said Mo, **grin**ning from ear to ear.

"What'd he say?" asked David.

"I remember every word," said Mo. "We were sitting by these **bush**es with these **weird**-looking yellow and red flowers and the man picked up a piece of paper right next to me!"

"She put it there," said Larry, "so that he'd have to come

near us to pick it up."

"It was my math test," said Mo. "It has my name on it! Luckily it didn't have my address."

"What did he say to you?" asked David.

Mo looked at David with wide, **frighten**ed eyes. "He said, 'Those are pretty flowers.'"

David stayed late in science class to help Mr. Lugano put away some **laboratory equipment** and **chemical**s. "Be careful not to drop anything," Mr. Lugano **warn**ed him.

"I won't," said David.

He didn't.

"You know, I was thinking," Larry said at lunch. "If you're afraid to go on a date with Tori—"

"I'm not afraid," said David. He lay on his back as he drank from a carton of lemonade.

"Well, anyway," said Larry. "I was thinking. It might be easier to ask her out if it was sort of like a double date.★"

"Huh?" said Mo.

"I was just thinking," Larry said to Mo. "Maybe you and I could pretend to be on a date, too. We wouldn't really be on a date. We'd just pretend to be on a date." He **adjust**ed his blue sunglasses. "Like, if David wants to put his arm around Tori, or something, he can **signal** me, and then I'll put my arm around you. I'll just be pretending, but Tori won't know that."

"Oh, well, sure, if it will make it easier for David," said Mo.

★ **double date** 두 쌍의 남녀가 함께 하는 데이트.

"Sure."

"So where do you want to go?" asked Larry.

"We could go to a movie," suggested Mo.

"Okay," said Larry. "A scary movie! That way Tori will want to hold David's hand or **grip** his arm or something."

"I'll grip your arm," said Mo. "But it won't **count**."

"Right," said Larry.

"It's still only a little past twelve," David **remind**ed them. "We have four more hours."

They never asked him, but actually he thought their "pretend" date was a good idea. That way, when he called up Tori he could just say something like, "Some friends of mine and I are going to a movie. You want to come along?"

That is—if the curse didn't strike first.

After school, Mo and Larry **stuck with him** to make sure he didn't **cheat**. "I'm not going to cheat," he **protest**ed. "Why would I cheat?"

They continued to plan their "pretend" date. They decided to see *The Tongue That Wouldn't Die!* It was scary and they figured it would also make Tori think about kissing.

"The curse may have already struck, and we don't even know it," said David.

"You'd know if—" Larry started, then stopped.

Roger, Scott, and Randy were hanging around the bike **rack** with three girls. Roger was with Leslie. Scott was with Ginger. Randy was with Tori.

David looked at Tori as she looked back at him. Then she

turned **abrupt**ly and said something to Randy.

David and his friends kept walking.

"You don't know that she likes Randy," said Mo. "She might just have been getting her bike."

"It was just a **coincidence** that she happened to be there when Randy was there," said Larry.

"She talked to him," said David.

"That doesn't mean anything," said Mo. "Maybe he was in her way. She probably said 'Get out of my way, **jerk**!' "

"You still have to ask her out," said Larry.

David realized that Mo and Larry didn't want anything to get in the way of their pretend date. "Unless the curse strikes," he said.

When they entered David's room, the clock radio next to his bed read 3:33 P.M.

"Three threes," said Larry. "That's lucky."

"I think the curse has already struck," said David. "I just haven't figured out how yet. It can be real **subtle** sometimes."

Larry and Mo didn't buy it.

"So, what do you want to do?" David asked.

"Nothing," said Mo. "We're just going to wait."

Ricky walked past David's door and **scowl**ed at David and his stoogy friends.

It was 3:45 P.M.

"We can go out back and throw the ball around," David suggested.

"No way," said Larry. "We're staying right here until four

seventeen."

"How about something to drink?" asked David. "I'll go make some lemonade."

Mo and Larry each put a hand on David's shoulder, holding him in place. "We're not thirsty," said Mo.

"You can't fight a curse," said David. "If it wants to strike it will strike whether we drink lemonade or not."

The clock read 3:57 P.M.

C'mon, curse, he thought. If you're going to strike, strike me now!

The time was 4:05 P.M.

"I have to go to the bathroom," said David.

"Not yet," said Mo.

"Look, do you want me to go in my pants?★ That could be part of the curse."

"I'll go with you," said Larry.

"I can go to the bathroom by myself."

"I'm going with you."

"Don't let him try anything," warned Mo.

Mo waited outside the bathroom door while Larry went in with David. He did what he had to do, **flush**ed the toilet, washed his hands, and started toward the door.

"Your **fly**," said Larry.

"I was just about to do that," said David. He zipped it up.

"So how'd it go?" Mo asked.

★ go in one's pants 바지에 실수를 하다.

"He tried to walk out with his zipper down," said Larry, "so you'd see his underwear!"

"I did not!" David exclaimed. "I can't believe you'd think I'd do that!"

They **escort**ed him back to his room as if he was some kind of **prisoner**. It was 4:13 P.M.

They watched the numbers change. 4:15 . . . 4:16. David looked up at the **ceiling** as if he hoped the **roof** would **cave in**.

4:17.

25

MO AND LARRY wanted David to call up Tori right then and there, but he **convinced** them that it would be better to call her up that night. Mo finally agreed that girls were more romantic at night.

"But if you **chicken out**," she warned, "don't even **bother** coming to school tomorrow."

David sat on his parents' bed and waited for 8:11 P.M. They had decided he'd call her then. They chose 8:11 P.M. because it would seem **spontaneous**. If he called her at exactly eight o'clock or exactly eight fifteen, Tori would know he'd been planning the call for a long time.

Sometimes you just have to do what your friends want you to do, David realized, no matter how terrible it is. He had finally learned that. It was the opposite of what everyone had always told him. Just say no, he had been told again and again. Don't let **peer** pressure make you do something you don't want to do. Be yourself. Just say no. If your friends don't like you for it, then they're not really your friends.

But he didn't have any other friends. He had said no to Roger and Randy. That was why they hated him.

Besides, Larry and Mo weren't asking him to do anything really bad. It wasn't as if they were asking him to take **drugs** or steal a car. They wanted him to ask out Tori Williams so that they could go out too. There's a difference between "just saying no" and letting your friends down.

It was more a matter of face. If he didn't call her up, he'd lose even more face. Besides, he wanted to go out with Tori. So what was the problem?

He was afraid that Tori Williams would just say no.

He got out the phone book from the nightstand next to his parents' bed and **thumb**ed through the pages until he got to Williams.

"HELLO."

"Hello, Tori, this is David."

"Oh, hi, David. I was just thinking about you."

"Really? What about me?"

"Oh, I don't think I should tell you *that*."

"Maybe I was thinking the same thing about you."

"Maybe."

"Well, anyway, the reason I called was—Would you like to go to a movie with me on Saturday night?"

"Sure, that sounds like fun."

Unfortunately, that conversation never happened—except in David's head.

"HELLO."

"Good evening, Miss Williams. This is Mr. Ballinger."

"Oh, well, make it quick, Ballinger. I'm expecting a call from Randy."

"Oh. Okay. Well, I, um, would be **delight**ed if you would **consent** to have tea with me on Saturday."

"What?"

"We don't have to have tea. I mean, some of my friends and I are going out to a movie and I thought maybe you'd like to come along."

"Are you asking me out on a date?"

"Yeah, sort of. Sure, why not?"

"Are you crazy? The only reason I talk to you is because I feel sorry for you. Why would somebody like me want to go out with a stooge like you? Be real, Curly!"

That conversation never happened either.

HE NEVER called her. There were more than two pages of people named Williams in the phone book.

He couldn't call up each and every one and ask if someone named Tori lived there. Surely Mo would understand that. What if there was another Tori Williams? What if he asked the wrong Tori Williams out on a date?

He decided he would just have to ask her for her phone

number tomorrow at school. Actually, the more he thought about it, the better he liked that idea. He'd ask her for her phone number, and then she'd ask him why he wanted it. Then he'd say because he wanted to call her up to ask her out on a date. If she gave him her phone number it would mean she wanted to go out with him. And if she didn't give him her phone number, then he wouldn't have to call her and be **reject**ed.

He put away the phone book and went into the **den** feeling a lot better about things. His mother and Ricky were watching television. Ricky turned and **scowl**ed at David.

"What's the matter, Ricky?" David asked **sarcastic**ally. "Wrestling not on?"

Elizabeth was playing with **block**s on the floor. She dropped a **circular** block through a circular shaped hole.

David, his mother, and his brother all **clap**ped their hands and told her what a good girl she was.

"How come I don't see Scott anymore?" David's mother asked.

David **shrug**ged. "I don't know," he **mutter**ed. "I guess we just have different interests."

"Yeah, Scott's not a stooge," said Ricky so only David could hear.

"Ba-ba," said Elizabeth.

"Bottle?" asked David.

"Ba-ba!" said Elizabeth.

"I'll get her some apple juice," said David's mother.

"That's okay," said David. "I'll get it."

142

He went into the kitchen and got the apple juice out of the **refrigerator**. As he poured it into Elizabeth's bottle he thought about Mrs. Bayfield. At least we're finally even, he decided, even if there never really was a curse. Everything that happened to her had now happened to him.

Except did that make them even, really? What if she didn't put a curse on him? What if it was just one coincidence after another? Then nothing that happened to him really **made up for** the **suffer**ing he had caused her.

He pictured her again, lying **helpless**ly on the ground, her face covered with lemonade, her legs in the air.

He stuck Elizabeth's bottle into the microwave for a few seconds to **take the chill off**. He started to screw on the **nipple** when the phone rang.

"Hello?" he said, answering it. "Hello?"

Nobody answered.

He hung up, then brought Elizabeth's bottle back to the den. "Here you go," he said, handing the bottle to her. "Good, fresh apple juice!"

"Ba-ba!" said Elizabeth as she took it from him. She turned it over above her head. The nipple fell off and the apple juice poured all over her face.

26

IT WASN'T the curse, David tried to tell himself later as he
sat on his bed. I just forgot to screw the nipple on Elizabeth's
bottle. It was because the phone rang. The phone had rung as I
was about to screw the nipple on and then I just forgot about it.
It could have happened to anyone.

He wondered who it was that called, then hung up. Maybe
it was Mrs. Bayfield. Maybe she called to make him forget
to screw the top on the bottle, so that it would pour all over
Elizabeth.

No, it couldn't be her, he realized. She only knew his first
name. There was no way she could know his phone number.

Of course, if she really was a **witch**, and if she could
somehow know the exact moment he'd be getting Elizabeth
apple juice, then she could also know his last name, phone
number, and who knows what else about him.

"Hey, David," said Ricky.

He turned and looked at his brother.

Ricky was standing in the **doorway**. His middle finger was raised and pointed at David.

FRIDAY MORNING David put on what he thought were his best and luckiest clothes. He needed all the luck he could get. Not only was he going to ask Tori for her phone number, but also he had to explain to Mo why he hadn't called Tori last night. Not to mention the fact that the curse was back.

"No blue jeans?" his mother said when she saw him.

He shrugged.

"Well, you look very nice," she said.

He wore a **baggy** pair of gray **drawstring** pants and a long-sleeved pullover shirt with no collar. The shirt had blue and white **horizontal** stripes. He kept the shirt on the outside of his baggy pants. He wore his regular dirty sneakers.

"You look like a stooge," Ricky said under his breath.

David ignored him. He didn't care what Ricky thought. All that mattered was what Tori thought.

When he got to school, Larry and Mo were waiting by his locker. He took a deep breath, then slowly headed toward them.

"So what'd she say?" asked Larry.

He took another breath.

"You better not say you didn't call her," warned Mo.

"I didn't call her," said David.

"I knew it!" said Mo. She turned to Larry. "I told you he'd **wimp** out."

chapter twenty-six

"I didn't know her phone number," David explained. "There were over two pages of Williamses in the phone book. What was I supposed to do, call each one?"

Mo shook her head in **disgust**.

"You should have found out her phone number before you went home yesterday," said Larry.

"How? I couldn't talk to her until four seventeen. Look, I'll talk to her today. I got it all **figured out**. I'll ask her for her phone number. If she gives it to me, then I'll know she wants me to call her up. If she doesn't give it to me, then it doesn't matter anyway."

Mo and Larry looked at him, unsure.

"By the way," David said, "the curse is back. Of course you don't care about that."

"What happened?" asked Larry.

He told them about the apple juice pouring onto Elizabeth's face. They both **giggle**d at the word *nipple*.

"Wait," said Larry when he had stopped giggling. "You said it was apple juice, right?"

David **nod**ded.

"Then you got nothing to worry about," said Larry. "So long as it wasn't lemonade. You just forgot to *screw the nipple.*" He and Mo giggled again.

David also told them about his brother giving him the finger.

"Look, you said you're going to ask her for her phone number?" asked Mo.

146

"Yeah."

"Then quit making excuses!"

David started to say something, then stopped as Roger and Randy walked past them. He could feel himself **tense** up as they **approach**ed, and then feel the tension leave his body as they passed.

"They seem to have stopped **hassling** us," said Larry. He laughed. "I think they're afraid of Mo."

Mo smiled.

"Yeah," David agreed. "She's our **watchdog**."

He didn't know why he said that.

Mo **flipped him off**, then turned and walked away.

"I'm sorry," David said to Larry. "But see, that proves the curse is back."

"It proves you're an asshole," said Larry.

"I didn't do anything," said David. "She's just super**sensitive**."

"Well, you just better ask Tori out," said Larry.

"Why? Just so you can go out on your *pretend* date with Mo? That's bullshit and you know it. You're just afraid to ask Mo out on a real date, so you're trying to **get a free ride** from me."

Larry flipped him off.

TORI WILLIAMS was already sitting at her desk when David entered Mr. MacFarland's class. She was having a very **lively** discussion with the girl who sat next to her, Lori Knapp. Tori was **gesturing** wildly about something and they were both laughing.

David planned the route to his desk so that he walked in front of her. He wanted to see how she'd **react** to him.

She didn't react at all. She just kept talking to Lori. As near as David could figure, they were talking about nose jobs.★

He sat down at his desk and **lean**ed back in his chair. It didn't matter anyway. He didn't have to ask her out anymore. She'd probably just flip him off too.

Is that it? he wondered. Is the whole world going to give me the finger? Is that my **punish**ment?

He imagined that for the rest of his life wherever he went, to the store, to the park, everyone who saw him would say, "Oh, you're David Ballinger," then flip him off. He'd get on a bus, and all the **passenger**s plus the driver would point their middle fingers at him. He'd go to a baseball game and suddenly the whole **crowd** would stand and shout, "Hey David Ballinger!" with their middle fingers raised high in the air.

His chair **toppled** over. He fell on his back with his legs in the air.

"Mr. Ballinger," said Mr. MacFarland.

He **scrambled** to his feet and quickly reset the chair. "Excuse me," he said.

After class he remained seated as he watched Tori walk out of the room. She never looked at him. He gathered his things and headed out. He was halfway to his math class when he stopped and hurried back the other way.

★ nose job 코 성형수술.

148

He slowed down when he saw Tori. He walked behind her for a while, watching her red hair **bounce** and flow across the back of her yellow shirt. He stepped up alongside her.

"Hi," he said.

Her green eyes **flash**ed as she turned and looked at him. "Hi," she answered.

They slowed their pace.

"Did you hurt yourself?" she asked.

"What? No." He shrugged. "It was just sort of **embarrass**ing." He looked at the underside of his elbow, where it had hit when he toppled over in his chair. There was a grayish mark on the shirt.

"That's a pretty shirt," she said.

"Thanks. It's my lucky shirt."

"It's nice. You look like a Greek **poet**."

He smiled. "You want to know why I wore my lucky shirt?" he asked.

"Why?"

They stopped walking. "Well, there was something I was going to ask you," he said. "Except it doesn't matter because now I don't have to ask you anymore."

"I wanted to ask you something, too," said Tori.

The bell rang. All around them kids **scurried** into classrooms.

"What'd you want to ask me?" asked David.

Tori smiled. "You tell me what you were going to ask me."

David folded his arms in front of him. "It doesn't really matter now," he said, "but, um, I was going to ask you if you had a phone."

"No!" she said **instantly**. She **blush**ed. "I mean yes, of course we have a phone, but, uh, I **hardly** ever use it. Why'd you want to know that?"

David shrugged. He was **taken aback** by her sudden **defensive**ness. "What'd you want to ask me?" he asked.

"Is Maureen your girlfriend?"

"Maureen?" he asked. "Mo? No. She's just a friend."

Tori pushed out one side of her mouth with her tongue. She looked toward a classroom, as if she needed to be going.

David uncrossed his arms, nervously put his hands behind his head, and **stretch**ed. "The reason I was wondering if you had a phone," he said, "was because I was just sort of wondering what your phone number was. I mean, I might want to call you up sometime to find out about homework or, you know, ask you out or something, and there's probably a lot of Williamses in the phone book."

Her green eyes were looking right at him. "You want my phone number?"

"I guess," he said. He stretched again. As he raised his arms the drawstring on his pants became **untied**, and his pants fell down.

In one motion he turned, pulled up his pants, and ran.

He didn't stop until he reached the **rust**y iron gate in front of Mrs. Bayfield's **mansion**.

150

27

THE GATE **creak**ed as David pushed it open. He walked slowly up the **path** to the house. The garden which had been **trample**d by Roger and Randy had been re**plant**ed with yellow and white chrysanthemums.★ The broken window next to the door had been fixed.

The rocking chair was **stuck** in the back corner of the **porch**. It seemed almost ghostlike, **teeter**ing **slight**ly as David stepped up the old wooden stairs onto the **splinter**ed porch.

The poor old woman is probably afraid to sit and rock anymore in her own front yard, he thought.

Poor old woman? He wondered how he could still think such things. She was a witch. Pants don't just fall down.

He approached the door and smiled uncertainly at the word

★ chrysanthemum 국화.

WELCOME printed across the old straw mat.*

He tried the doorbell, although he could tell by looking at it that it probably wouldn't work. It didn't. It **practically** fell off the wall when he pushed it.

He had to pull open a **torn** screen door* so he could **knock** on the heavy wood door behind it. There was an **odd**-shaped door knocker. He knocked a couple of times with his **fist**, but that didn't seem to make much of a noise, so he lifted the heavy metal door knocker. He then realized it was in the shape of a **shrunken** head. He knocked it twice against the door, then quickly stepped back.

The screen door **bang**ed shut in front of him.

He didn't know what he would say when Mrs. Bayfield opened the door—if she opened the door. All he could do was tell her he was sorry and **beg** her forgiveness.

He heard movement inside the house, then the **doorknob** turned and the door opened a few inches. Mrs. Bayfield **peer**ed out at him from under a safety chain.*

"I'm sorry," he said. "I'm really sorry. I know I should have said I was sorry earlier, instead of pouring lemonade on my head, and I'm sorry I didn't. I guess I just didn't believe you put a **curse** on me, but that doesn't matter. I should have said I was sorry anyway, whether or not you put a curse on me. The curse

---

★ straw mat 다다미. 속에 짚을 두껍게 넣고 위에는 돗자리를 대어 단단히 꿰맨 것으로 마루에 까는 매트.
✻ screen door 곤충의 침입을 방지하기 위해 다는 망을 친 문.
✼ safety chain 현관문 안쪽에 부착되는 사슬. 문을 약간 열어 방문자를 확인을 할 수 있게 한다.

152

shouldn't have anything to do with it. Even if my pants didn't fall down. I shouldn't have even been here **in the first place.** I never should have pointed my finger at you, whether you know what it means or not, although I guess you probably do. I thought it would make me popular. But I never wanted to hurt you. You have to believe that. It's because I have no face."

He didn't know if anything he said **made sense.** Mrs. Bayfield didn't say a word.

"What else can I say?" he asked. "I'm sorry. What do you want me to say?"

The door closed.

There was a **click**ing sound and then the door opened wide. Mrs. Bayfield was wearing a plain brown-knit dress and she **lean**ed on a plain wooden **cane.** She looked older than he remembered. For some reason it made him glad when he noticed that she had on the same red high-top sneakers.

"Come in," she said.

He stepped inside.

Although the outside of the house was old and **run-down,** the inside was beautifully and **lavish**ly **decorate**d. The floor to the entryway was covered with green and white marble tile, and the walls were covered with a rich red and black cloth. A large **oval** mirror **encase**d in an **ornate** gold frame hung on the wall in front of him.

He smiled **mocking**ly at his "lucky" clothes as he saw himself in the mirror.

"You look like a Greek **poet**," said Mrs. Bayfield.

The smile left his face. He turned and looked at her in **awe**. He shouldn't have been surprised. He already knew she was a witch. At least he thought he knew that, but those last words erased any **doubt**s he still might have had.

It was exactly what Tori had said to him—before his pants fell down.

Felicia Bayfield **obvious**ly had seen and heard everything that had happened to him. She'd seen his pants fall down. Of course she probably saw him put on his pants every morning, too.

He got even more proof, not that he needed it, as he passed a small table with a telephone. Next to the phone was a pad of paper with DAVID BALLINGER written on it. Under his name was his phone number.

He nodded as he looked at it. So she was the one who called him last night.

She led him into the living room. He felt his eyes **widen** as he looked at all the strange and beautiful masks hanging on the walls.

He sat down on the edge of the **couch** and **stare**d at them. Some of the masks were very odd; faces with three eyes or faces that were half black and half white. There was one that looked like it was part lion and part human, although it was impossible to tell where the lion stopped and the human started.

But the **eerie**st ones looked like real faces. He couldn't tell what they were made of. They seemed to have too much **texture** to be paper or plastic. There was a woman with a double **chin**, a man with a deep **scar**, and one mask in particular that he couldn't stop looking at. It was the face of a very **ordinary** man with wire-**rim**med glasses and a tiny **birthmark** on his **cheek**. The mask **extend**ed just below the man's chin, so that there was the very top of a tie, and just above his head to the very bottom of a hat. David had the feeling that if you removed the hat and tie, the face would just **dissolve** away.

He turned his eyes away from the masks to the **wrinkle**d face of Mrs. Bayfield. She was sitting in a large over**stuff**ed armchair across from him.

"What happened to your friends?" she asked.

"Oh, you mean Roger, Scott, and Randy? They're not my friends. Scott used to be my best friend but not anymore. Roger and Randy were never my friends, not even then. They're the ones you should have cursed. Not me. I mean, I'm not saying I wasn't **partly** to blame, but they're the ones who knocked you over and poured lemonade on your head and stole your cane. Why'd you pick me? I just sort of went along with them."

"I wonder . . . ." said Mrs. Bayfield. "Who is more to blame? The leaders or the followers?"

"Isn't there anything I can do?" David **plead**ed. "I still have my whole life ahead of me! Just tell me what I have to do, and I'll do it!" He threw up his hands. "Or am I just going to be cursed for the rest of my life? Can you tell me that? Do I have to spend my whole life wondering when my pants are going to fall down?"

Mrs. Bayfield's green eyes sparkled as she smiled. "Isn't that what life is all about?" she asked. "We all pretend we're such important, **dignified** people. We become doctors or lawyers or artists. Hello. How are you? Let's have a barbecue on the Fourth of July.★ But really we all know that at any moment our pants might fall down."

"There was this girl," said David.

"Of course."

"I know you know," said David. "It's just that I think she might have liked me. Did she? Do you know that? Can you tell me? I know it doesn't matter anymore, but can you tell me what she would have said if my pants didn't fall down?"

Mrs. Bayfield pushed out one side of her face with her tongue.

David shook his head. "Never mind," he said. "It doesn't matter anyway. I can never face her again. How can I even go back to school? Everyone will know about it. And then my brother will hear about it at his school. He already thinks I'm the biggest stooge on earth."

"Bring me back my cane," said Mrs. Bayfield.

David looked up. "And then you'll remove the curse?"

"Bring me my cane," she repeated.

★ **Fourth of July** 미국 독립 선언 기념일.

156

28

HE HEADED in no particular direction as he walked away from Mrs. Bayfield's house. He couldn't go back to school and it was too early to go home.

He thought about running away. He could hitchhike★ to San Francisco, then **stow** away on a boat to China. By the time anyone found him it would be too late. They'd have to give him a job **mop**ping the **deck**, or was it called **swab**bing the deck?

Of course he knew he would never do that. Besides, he couldn't run away from the curse. It would follow him wherever he went, **dump**ing lemonade on his head and pulling down his pants. Somehow he'd have to get the cane from Roger Delbrook.

Maybe he could buy it from him? He had more than five hundred dollars in the bank. He **figure**d he could probably get

★ **hitchhike** 히치하이크. 지나가는 자동차를 얻어 타는 일.

the cane for no more than fifty.

He imagined their conversation. *Hey, Roger, I got a deal for you,* he'd say.

What do you want, Ballinger? asks Roger.

You know that cane you took from old Buttfield? I'll give you ten bucks for it.

Go to hell, Ballinger.

I'm not kidding. I'll give you ten dollars for it. Make it fifteen.

I wouldn't give you the cane for a hundred dollars, asshole!

*All right, twenty dollars, but that's my final **offer**.*

You really want it? You can have it for fifty!

Twenty-five.

Forty.

Thirty.

Thirty-five.

Okay, thirty-five.

He'd give Roger the money and Roger would give him the cane.

*Here's the cane. Take it and stick it up your **ass**!*

Thanks.

It seemed like a good plan. It was certainly worth thirty-five dollars to **get rid of** the curse.

Or he could steal it.

He had thought he was walking in no particular direction, but looking up, he **discover**ed he was at the corner of Commonwealth Circle. Roger lived at the end of the street. David had never been inside Roger's house, but he knew where he lived. His house was at the **cul-de-sac** at the end of the **block**.

Both of Roger's parents probably worked, so there was probably no one home right now. The cane was probably just **stuck** inside Roger's closet.

He walked down the street. It was amazingly quiet. There might not have been anyone home in any of the houses.

With his hands in his pockets, he walked around the circle of the cul-de-sac. He just wanted to get a better look at Roger's house. He had nothing better to do. He had no **intention** of **break**ing **in**.

But if he was going to break in, how would he do it? First he'd have to ring the doorbell to make sure nobody was home. And then if there was nobody home?

At the side of the house there was a fence with a gate leading to the backyard. He could just walk through the gate, or, if it was locked, **hop** the fence. Once in the backyard, no one would be able to see him from the street. He would just have to find an open window.

Or he could break a window. He smiled. Roger broke Mrs. Bayfield's window. It would only be fair. Roger stole Mrs. Bayfield's cane. Now he could break Roger's window and steal back the cane. **Might as well trample** some flowers while he was at it.

Of course he wasn't really going to do that. He was just **kill**ing **time** until he could go home. He walked toward the Delbrooks' front door, just to see if anybody was home.

He tried to think of what he'd say if somebody answered.

He could say he was selling magazines. No, that was too **complicated**. If he heard someone coming, he'd just run away. No harm, no **foul**.

He rang the doorbell.

No one answered the door.

Just to make certain, he rang the bell again. He also knocked loudly on the door with the side of his fist.

Nobody was home.

He stepped backward off the **stoop** away from the door and looked around. The street was still empty. He **casual**ly headed toward the side of the house.

There was a small chain sticking through a hole in the tall wooden gate. He **tug**ged at the chain. It was locked.

He stepped back. The fence was about seven feet tall. He took a few more steps backward, then **untie**d the **drawstring** on his pants and retied it, tight.

He ran at the fence and jumped. He **grab**bed the top of the gate with his hands as his feet kicked against the side trying to get some sort of **traction**. He managed to get his right elbow up and then swung his right leg over.

"Hey! What are you doing?"

He looked back to see a little kid running toward him. It was Roger's brother, Glen.

David was half on, half off the top of the gate. "My ball went over the fence," he said. He hopped back down to the ground. "I rang the doorbell but nobody was home."

"I know who you are," said Glen. "You're Ricky's brother."

"I was just getting my ball," said David. He didn't know why he was even **bother**ing to explain himself to a fifth grader. "Forget it!" He started to walk away.

"Stooge!"

He stopped and turned around. "What'd you call me?"

"Stooge!" Glen said **scornful**ly. "You're the Big Stooge and Ricky is the Little Stooge. That's what everyone calls him."

David took a step toward him.

"You know what Ricky said?" asked Glen. "He said The Three Stooges were highly respected in their field!" He laughed. "He said it was a **compliment** to be called a stooge!"

"I'm **warn**ing you," said David as he took another step toward Glen.

Glen raised his **fist**s. "You want to fight?" he asked. "I'll fight you. I could **beat** you up just like I beat up Ricky."

David stopped. He didn't know what to do. He couldn't very well fight a little kid. "What are you doing home from school?" he demanded.

"Half day," said Glen, his fists in the air. "Teachers' meeting."

David **glare**d at him, then **sigh**ed **disgust**edly, trying to show his **contempt**.

"What's the matter?" asked Glen. "You afraid to fight a fifth grader?"

"I got better things to do than **mess with** a little kid like you," said David, turning away.

"Stooge!" shouted Glen. "Wait till I tell my brother. Wait till I tell my brother you were afraid to fight a fifth grader! And

I **bet** there's no ball back there, either. Wait till I tell my brother you were—"

David spun around. "You can tell your brother . . . You can tell your brother that I think he's a **sack** of dogshit! Tell him that. Tell your **pissant** brother that I'll be back here tomorrow, if he wants to do anything about it. Tell him I want the snake-head cane, too. You got all that or do you want me to write it down for you? Tell him David Ballinger will be back tomorrow at noon to get the snake-head cane and that he better be here!"

He turned and **strode** away, leaving Glen Delbrook with his mouth hanging open.

29

LARRY CLARKSDALE'S number wasn't listed in the phone book, but David was able to get it from Information.

"What happened to you?" Larry asked after his sister called him to the phone. "Where'd you go?"

"You didn't hear about it?" asked David.

"No. What?"

"The curse **struck**."

"What happened?" Larry asked **sarcastic**ally. "Did you step on a flower?" He was obviously still a little mad from this morning.

David was glad that at least the whole school hadn't heard about his pants falling down. Or maybe everyone heard about it—except Larry.

"It struck," he said simply. "I can't tell you how, but it was **definite**ly the curse. I had to leave school." He paused for effect. "I went back to Mrs. Bayfield's house."

He thought he heard Larry **gasp**.

He told Larry what Mrs. Bayfield said, and then what happened when he tried to steal the cane.

"Why?" Larry asked when he was through.

"What do you mean, 'Why'?" asked David.

"You don't really believe in that **stuff**, do you?" asked Larry. "Curses? Witches?"

"If you knew what happened today, you'd believe," said David. "Besides, you're the one who talked about boomerang curses. You're the one who made me pour lemonade on my head!"

"But I didn't tell you to call Roger Delbrook a sack of dogshit," said Larry. "That's just asking for trouble."

"But—"

"Anyway, I never lived in Australia," Larry admitted. "I made that up."

David felt a **sink**ing feeling in his stomach. Larry had been his one hope. "What about Japan?" he asked.

"I never lived outside the U.S. Hey, but don't tell Mo, okay? She thinks I'm a man of the world."

"Then you don't know kung fu?" asked David.

"I had a couple of lessons when we lived in Indianapolis," said Larry.

"You said you had a black belt."

"I do. It goes with my gray **slacks**."

"Oh great," said David. "I was hoping you'd help me tomorrow. I'll fight Roger—I have to do that—but I was hoping you'd keep his friends away in case they tried anything." He **sigh**ed. "What about Carmelita?" he asked. "You didn't live in Venezuela, either?"

"I bought those pictures from a guy for five bucks," said Larry. "I think he lived in Venezuela."

"Thanks a lot!" said David. "You complain about how hard it is to make friends, but then I try to be your friend and all you do is lie to me. Then, when I really need you, you let me down. Some friend!"

"Me?" asked Larry. "You're the one who didn't call up Tori when you said you would. And then you called Mo a dog. Man, you're lucky you didn't go back to school today. She was ready to kill you. And then the only reason you call me up isn't to **apologize** but because you want my help. No way! I'm not going to fight your battles for you. You got yourself into this, not me. I mean, now who's trying to **get a free ride**?"

"Forget it!" **snap**ped David. "I should have known better than to ask *you* to help a friend."

"Friend? You're not a friend. You're a **leech**. No wonder Scott hates you!"

"You've got no face," said David. "Only a pair of ugly blue sunglasses."

"You're a butthead."

David heard Larry **slam** down the phone. "And you're a dipshit," he said into the dead air.

He walked down the hall. The door to Ricky's room was open. David could see him sitting at his desk, probably doing homework.

Big stooge, little stooge. It was one thing for Roger and Scott to call him a stooge, but it wasn't fair that Ricky was the little stooge. Big stooge, little stooge. It **gnaw**ed at his insides whenever he thought about it. Even if there was no curse or cane, he'd have to fight Roger for that.

Ricky turned around and looked at him.

"Hi," said David. "You want help with your homework or anything?"

"Go blow your nose, **snot**face!" said Ricky. David continued down the hall. Go blow your nose, snotface! He wondered if one of the other fifth graders said that to Ricky today.

Actually, he suddenly did feel like he needed to blow his nose. Maybe it was the power of **suggest**ion.

He didn't **dare** let Ricky hear him. He went through his parents' bedroom to their bathroom and closed the door.

It seemed so **hopeless**. Roger was bigger and stronger than he was. Plus, Roger knew he was coming so he'd probably have all his friends there too.

It's me against the world. I have no friends left. My brother hates me. I'm cursed. I can never talk to Tori again.

He looked at himself in the bathroom mirror and smiled. A strange feeling of confidence came over him.

He had nothing left to lose.

30

"I CLOSED my eyes," said Tori Williams.

She was standing at his front door. It was ten thirty, Saturday morning. He had been playing solitaire★ as he **anxious**ly waited for twelve o'clock, when he heard the doorbell ring. He went to the door and there she was.

"You asked me for my phone number," she said. "I closed my eyes as I tried to remember it. I can remember things better when my eyes are closed. When I opened my eyes, you were gone."

He **stared** at her for a second. Or maybe it was a minute.

"Aren't you going to invite me in, Mr. Ballinger?" she asked. "It's not polite to leave a lady standing out in the cold."

"Please come in, Miss Williams. Would you care for a cup of tea?"

★ solitaire 솔리테르. 혼자서 하는 카드놀이.

"Thank you."

He led her into the kitchen.

"Do you have any herb tea?" she asked.

"I don't know. I don't think so. I'll check."

He found a brown bag of tea way in the back of the **cabinet** behind the coffee, decaffeinated coffee,★ regular tea, coffee filters, paper plates, and birthday candles. "Chamomile✳ tea?" he asked, pronouncing it like it was spelled. He'd never heard of it before.

"Cam-o-meel," said Tori. "It's good."

It wasn't in tea bags and David didn't know how to brew loose tea,✳ so Tori made it. She used a Japanese teapot that David and Ricky had once given their mother on Mother's Day. As far as David could remember, it had never been used before.

They sat next to each other at the kitchen **counter** and **sip**ped their tea. David added some honey to his. It didn't taste too bad—kind of like sweet grass. Her eyes **flash**ed at him over her raised teacup.

He looked at the clock on the stove. It was ten to eleven. He set down his cup. "You're going to think this is really weird," he said.

"What?"

"I don't know how to begin." He smiled. "**Fourscore** and

★ **decaffeinated coffee** 카페인을 줄인 커피.

✳ **chamomile** 캐모마일. 쌍떡잎식물 초롱꽃목 국화과의 풀로, 차로 마시거나 기름을 얻어 사용한다.

✳ **loose tea** 깡통 등 방습용기에 다량으로 넣은 홍차.

seven years ago—"

Tori laughed.

"Do you know that lady, uh, Mrs. Bayfield?"

Tori **swallow**ed her tea. "Yes. She's—"

"She's a **witch!**" said David.

Her eyes **widen**ed. "She is?"

"I'm not kidding. She put a **curse** on me. That's why those things have been happening to me, like what happened yesterday when I asked you for your phone number."

"I closed my eyes," said Tori.

"Well, I just want you to know it wasn't my fault. I guess **in a way** it was my fault, but not in the way you'd think. It all started about three weeks ago. I used to **hang out** with Scott, Roger, and Randy."

He **notice**d Tori's face **redden** slightly when he mentioned Randy's name.

"Have you ever seen Mrs. Bayfield's snake-head cane?" he asked.

"Uh, I think so," said Tori. "It was stolen, wasn't it?" She took another sip of tea.

He wondered how she knew that. He wondered what she was doing here. It suddenly **occur**red to him that Randy might have sent her as part of some kind of joke. Or maybe as a spy.

"I helped steal it," he said.

She raised her **eyebrow**s.

He told Tori what happened. How they **knock**ed Mrs. Bayfield over and stole her **cane**, but the whole time he had the feeling that Tori already knew all about it.

"At the time I thought it was a mean thing to do to a poor old lady," he said. "You know, what if it was her only cane and she couldn't walk without it? Little did I know . . . ." He shook his head. "I really didn't do anything bad to her, except for **giving her the finger**, which really isn't so bad when you think about it. Mostly I just sort of stood around." He **shrug**ged. "But I guess followers are just as much to blame as leaders."

"What did Randy do?" asked Tori.

"Randy? He was the one who pulled her rocking chair over."

"So then what happened?" asked Tori.

"She put a curse on me. I know it sounds crazy, but everything that happened to her started happening to me!" He told her about throwing the baseball through the window and about the apple juice pouring on Elizabeth's face. "Remember when I fell over in my chair in social studies?"

"Yes!" **whisper**ed Tori. "Twice." She put her hand over her mouth. "Was that the curse?"

David **nod**ded. "Just like she had been knocked over in her rocking chair. And I guess you probably heard about the beaker I broke in science."

She nodded. Her mouth was hidden behind her cup, but he thought she was smiling.

"It wasn't my fault," he explained. "It was the curse. Roger broke her **pitcher** of lemonade, so she broke my pitcher."

"She must be a witch," Tori said **conclusive**ly.

He couldn't tell if she really believed that or if she was just playing along. "She really is," he said. "She steals people's faces. She has them hanging all over the walls of her house. Somehow she manages to keep them **preserved**."

"The lemonade!" **exclaim**ed Tori.

"Huh?"

"It probably wasn't really lemonade. It was face juice!"

"Uh, maybe," said David.

"Lucky you didn't drink any," said Tori.

He nodded. He told her about seeing Mrs. Bayfield's underwear. "And then, well, you know what happened yesterday when I was talking to you."

"I closed my eyes," she **remind**ed him.

He smiled. "Well, even if you didn't see what happened, she saw. She sees and hears everything I do!"

"She does? How do you know?"

"Well, I don't know if you remember but, um, yesterday you said I looked like a Greek **poet**."

Tori **blush**ed.

"After I left you, I ran to see her. To try to **beg** her to remove the curse. The first thing she said to me was, 'You look like a Greek poet.' It was her way of telling me she'd been watching me the whole time."

Again, David thought he saw Tori smile behind her cup. Why did he have the feeling she knew something he didn't?

"I wonder if she's watching us right now," Tori whispered. She looked around **suspicious**ly.

"Probably. There's nothing we can do about it." He **glance**d at the clock. "So anyway, now I have to get the cane and bring it back to her so she'll remove the curse."

"Did she tell you that?"

He nodded.

"She said she'd remove the curse if you returned the cane?" For the first time, Tori seemed **genuine**ly surprised.

"Yes," he said. Then he took a sip of tea.

"Hmmm," said Tori.

Ricky was coming down the hall. David watched him **out of the corner of his eye**. The last thing he needed was for Ricky to **make** some **crack** about his brother the stooge, or his stoogy girlfriend.

Ricky stopped and stared at Tori. He walked into the kitchen.

"Hi," she **greet**ed him.

"Hi," said Ricky, still staring.

David introduced them. "Tori, this is my brother, Ricky. Ricky—Tori."

"Would you like some chamomile tea?" Tori offered.

David closed his eyes. He could just imagine what his brother was thinking.

"Okay," said Ricky.

"Get a cup," said Tori.

Ricky got a teacup and sat down at the counter on the other side of Tori. He reached for the teapot, but Tori picked it up first. "It's bad luck to pour your own tea," she said as she poured it for him.

He took a sip, then **made a face**.

"Do you want some honey in it?" she asked.

"Did you put honey in your tea?" asked Ricky.

"No, I like it plain."

"I don't want honey," he said. He took another sip of tea. "It's good." He smiled at Tori.

David watched, amazed. Ricky **obvious**ly didn't think Tori was a stooge. He glanced at the clock on the stove. It was twenty-five past eleven.

"Like this," said Tori. She held her teacup in her first two fingers. Her **pinky** was sticking straight out.

Ricky **daintily** picked up his teacup.

They both laughed.

The doorbell rang.

David and Ricky looked at each other.

"Somebody get that!" shouted their father.

"I'll get it," Ricky said **reluctant**ly. He took another sip of chamomile tea, then stood up and headed for the door.

David and Tori smiled at each other like they were sharing some secret joke, except David didn't know what the joke was.

Ricky returned, followed by Larry, Mo, and a little brown and gray dog that Mo had on a **leash**.

It wasn't much bigger than a puppy, with one ear up and the other down.

"Oh, how cute!" exclaimed Tori.

Larry and Mo stared at her for a second, then looked **quizzical**ly at David.

He shrugged.

Larry pointed at the dog with his **thumb**, smiled, and said, "Killer."

"I got him at the **pound**," said Mo, **kneel**ing down to pet her dog. "I wanted to get a big, mean dog, but"—she **rub**bed Killer's head—"if nobody took him they would have **execut**ed him."

Killer **lick**ed her face.

"Would you like some chamomile tea?" Tori offered.

"Barf," said Mo.

Tori laughed.

"No, it's really good," said Ricky.

"So, uh," said Larry, "we'll go with you to fight Roger. If you still want. I mean, if you're going to get beat up, I **might as well** get beat up too." He smiled and **adjust**ed his blue sunglasses. "What are best friends for?"

David smiled. "Thanks, buddy," he said. "Thanks, Mo."

"I'm not just doing it for you," said Mo. "I'm doing it for me, too. I'm sick of those"—she looked at Ricky—"aardvarks.★"

"You're going to fight Roger Delbrook?" asked Tori.

"If I have to," said David. "He has the cane."

"I'm going too," she **declar**ed.

"Me too!" exclaimed Ricky.

David looked at his brother. "I don't—"

"Glen'll be there," said Ricky. "I want another shot at Glen Delbrook!"

★ **aardvark** 땅돼지. 긴 혀로 개미를 핥아먹는 아프리카 남부의 동물.

31

THEY FINISHED their tea, everybody who had to went to the bathroom, and at a quarter to twelve they headed for Roger Delbrook's house.

Ricky and Tori held hands. David was glad that Ricky liked Tori, although he would have liked to have been the one holding her hand. After all, he was the one who was about to get his face broken.

"Wait," said Mo.

Everyone stopped while Killer did some business in the middle of the **sidewalk**.

"Okay," said Mo.

"You should clean that up," said David.

"Why?"

"Someone might step in it."

"So?"

David stared at her. He didn't know why he was getting

into this now.

"You clean it up," said Mo.

"I'll clean it up," said Tori. Using a stick, she pushed Killer's **droppings** off the sidewalk and into the **bush**es.

David felt foolish. "I guess we're just a little **tense**," he said.

"Yeah," said Mo. "Hey," she said, trying to sound **upbeat**, "we got nothing to worry about. Roger's the one who should be worrying!"

"Yeah!" Larry joined in, trying to sound **enthusiastic**.

"And Glen!" said Ricky.

"They're probably **pee**ing in their pants right now!" said Mo.

Ricky laughed.

They continued on to the Delbrooks' house. Tori held Ricky's hand again. "It's the house at the end of this street," Ricky said when they got to Commonwealth Circle, letting everyone know that he knew the way; that he wasn't just **tagging along**.

They walked to the end of the **cul-de-sac**.

"Wait here," said David. He walked alone to the front door.

The house seemed quiet and dark, as if no one was home. Maybe Roger's afraid of me, he thought. Yeah, right.

He was about to ring the bell, then he stopped and pounded loudly on the door with his **fist**.

He waited.

"Sorry, we don't want any," said Roger, opening the door. His friends laughed.

"Hey, **Curly**, zip your **fly**!" said Ginger.

They were all there: Randy, Scott, Alvin, Leslie, Ginger, and

Glen.

"I've come for the cane," said David, trying to keep his voice from **quiver**ing.

"Well, you're not getting the cane," said Roger in a **whiny**, **mocking** voice.

His friends laughed.

"Do yourself a favor, Ballinger," said Scott. "Go home."

David **glare**d at his former best friend. "This has nothing to do with you, *Scotty*," he said. "So just keep your kiss-**ass**★ nose out of it."

Scott reddened. He started to reply, but seemed to **gag** on his words. He laughed **scornful**ly.

"Is this what you want?" asked Leslie, holding up the cane with the two heads and four green eyes. She handed it to Roger.

"I'll fight you for it," David **challeng**ed Roger. "Winner gets the cane."

Roger laughed. "Why should I fight for it?" he asked. "I already have it."

His friends laughed again.

David didn't know what to do. He had worried about a lot of things **throughout** his **sleepless** night, but it never **occur**red to him that Roger just wouldn't fight him. "You chicken?" he challenged.

Roger laughed. "That's me," he said, smiling.

David **flip**ped **him off**.

★ **kiss-ass** '아첨하다', '알랑거리다'라는 뜻의 'kiss one's ass'를 바꾼 표현.

The smile left Roger's face. "Don't do that," he **warn**ed.

David kept his middle finger pointed at Roger as he stepped back off the front **stoop**.

Roger handed the cane to Randy. "You better take it back," he said, stepping outside.

Take it back? David wondered. How would he do that—keep his middle finger down and raise the other four?

"What are you smiling at?" demanded Roger.

He hadn't realized he was smiling, but now he smiled even wider, keeping his finger pointed right at Roger's nose.

"Look, he brought his *gang*," Alvin said, laughing as he followed Roger outside.

"Some gang," said Roger. "Three big stooges, one little stooge, and—" He stopped and looked at Randy.

Randy reddened.

David kept his finger raised as he glanced at Tori.

Roger's fist **bang**ed into his ear. He **stumble**d backward but didn't fall. A second punch hit him in the side of the neck.

He held his arms in front of his face for **protect**ion as he tried to get his balance so he could fight back. Roger's fist **smash**ed through his arms into his nose.

David swung weakly back at Roger. He heard Mo cheering, "C'mon, David, get 'm!" as Roger **slug**ged him in the stomach.

Roger **grab**bed David's shirt collar with his left hand and hit him in the face again and again with the front and back of his right fist. David felt like a rag doll,* unable to protect himself or fight back. At last his shirt collar **rip**ped off in Roger's hand,

178

and he fell **dizzily** to the ground.

As he looked up at Roger he realized something he wished he had realized a lot sooner. He didn't know how to fight. He didn't know how to **defend** himself or even throw a punch . . . .

RICKY **FLUNG** himself at Glen, and the two boys fell to the ground. They rolled around on the grass, grabbing and **claw**ing at each other . . . .

"HEY, MO, is that your sister?" asked Alvin, pointing at Killer.

Mo pushed him. "You afraid to fight a girl?" she challenged.

"No," said Alvin. He **slam**med his open hand into her nose and mouth.

She fell to the ground. Alvin brought his leg back, like he was about to kick her, but stopped. "Aw, she's crying," he said.

Larry took off his blue sunglasses . . . .

DAVID REALIZED something else, too. He could stand the pain. Sure, it hurt, but *not that much*. He pulled himself to his feet and **charge**d wildly at Roger . . . .

RICKY HAD Glen in a headlock✳ and kept tightening his **grip** as Glen **helpless**ly kicked his legs . . . .

SCOTT HAD one arm around Ginger and the other around

★ rag doll 헝겊으로 만든 인형.

✳ headlock 헤드록. 레슬링에서 두 팔로 상대의 머리를 안아서 죄는 기술.

Leslie. Tori slowly walked toward them . . . .

"YEEE-AHHH!" shouted Larry, jumping in front of Alvin. He tried to remember everything he learned in his kung fu class in Indianapolis. His hands were like steel plates,★ but his arms and legs were **fluid** like water. He was in tune with his center of balance.

"What are you supposed to be?" asked Alvin.

Larry kicked him in the stomach . . . .

GLEN TWISTED out of the headlock, **jam**med his elbow into Ricky's side, and climbed on top of him. Ricky kept a hand on Glen's face, trying to push him back. Glen punched him in the eye, but it was with his left hand and not very hard . . . .

TORI PUSHED her way past Scott and continued on toward Randy, who was sitting on the front stoop holding the cane in his **lap.** She sat down next to him . . . .

DAVID **DUCK**ED under Roger's flying fist and charged into him. They both fell to the ground. David quickly **lunge**d on top of him and punched Roger as hard as he could in the side of his face. Roger **wince**d with pain . . . .

KILLER SAT in Mo's lap, **lick**ing the tears off her face.

★ **steel plate** 강판. 저탄소강으로 만들어진 판재.

Larry tried to kick Alvin again, but this time Alvin caught Larry's foot in **midair**. Larry had the wind knocked out of him as he fell hard on his back. Alvin **dragged** him across the yard . . . .

ROGER PUSHED David off of him and punched him in his already **bloody** nose. He grabbed David's curly hair, pulled him into the bushes, and ground his face into the dirt . . . .

TORI AND RANDY stared into each other's eyes. Randy shrugged his shoulders . . . .

ALVIN DRAGGED Larry right through the middle of a bush, then dropped him in the dirt next to where David was lying . . . .

RICKY HAD Glen **pin**ned down. "You **give up?**"

"No," Glen **groan**ed.

"You give up?" Ricky asked again, pushing Glen's **chin** back, **stretch**ing his neck.

"No!" Glen **gasp**ed.

Roger kicked Ricky in the side of the head.

The next thing Ricky knew, he was lying on the ground next to Glen.

"You better leave my brother alone," Roger warned, standing over him . . . .

LARRY **COUGH**ED.

David lay with his head in the dirt. He wasn't ready to lift it yet. He just needed to lie there. He closed his eyes.

"Oh, I think I'm going to throw up," Larry **moan**ed. He coughed again.

David's head ached as he pulled himself up to his knees. He **spat** some dirt out of his mouth.

Larry pulled himself up too. They stumbled across the yard. David wiped his face on his **sleeve**, then looked at the blood and dirt on his shirt.

Mo handed Larry his blue sunglasses. "You were wonderful!" she said, **beam**ing.

Tori walked up behind them and **slip**ped her arm through David's. "Shall we take our leave, Mr. Ballinger?" she asked. She was holding the snakehead cane . . . .

RICKY AND GLEN sat next to each other on the ground.

"You had me," Glen admitted. "Until my brother went and kicked you. I can't believe he'd do that."

Ricky shrugged. His head still **throb**bed.

"Your brother's girlfriend is pretty," said Glen.

Ricky **nod**ded.

"Your brother's okay, too," Glen added.

"He's the best!" said Ricky . . . .

ROGER SHOOK his head as he looked down at Randy, who was still sitting on the front stoop. "Why the hell did you give her the cane?" he demanded.

"She doesn't even like you," said Leslie. "She likes David."

182

"Tell me something I don't know," said Randy . . . .

"WE SHOWED them!" **declare**d Larry behind his blue sunglasses as they headed away from the Delbrook house.

"You better believe it!" echoed Mo. "That's the last time anyone **messes with** us."

"Did you see my kung fu?" asked Larry. "I learned that in Japan. Would you believe I only had one lesson? Man, if I just had a couple more lessons! But still, my first kick—*whap!*—right in his **gut**. Alvin now knows what it's like to feel the foot of Larry Clarksdale!"

"That's right!" said Mo.

"You **stood up to** him too, Mo," said Larry, "until he sucker-punched★ you."

"I may have been down," Mo said, "but I wasn't out."

"You just had to watch Killer," said Ricky.

Mo smiled at Ricky. "Right," she said. "I like the way you handled Glen."

"I did all right," said Ricky. "And he knows it. I mean, Glen's not really a bad guy. He's just got a **rotten** brother."

"Well, I have to admit Roger probably **got the better of me**," said David, **limp**ing on the cane. "But I got in one good punch, and he's going to remember that for a long, long time."

"Better believe it," said Larry.

"No one **picks on** my brother and gets away with it!" Ricky

---

★ sucker-punch 불시의 타격.

said **triumphantly**.

"Or mine," said David.

"We went after the cane," said Larry, "and we got it!"

David raised the cane into the air and they all cheered.

"Couldn't have done it without Tori," said Mo. "She just walked right up to Randy and took the cane from him. He never knew what hit him."

Tori smiled. She karate-**chop**ped the air in front of her. "Broke his heart right in two," she said with just a **trace** of sadness in her voice.

32

TORI'S AND David's hands almost but not quite touched as their arms swung back and forth. David could still feel the **spot** on his arm where Tori touched him and said, "Shall we take our leave, Mr. Ballinger?" That one spot of pleasure more than **made up for** all the spots of pain that covered the rest of him.

He looked at her walking beside him. She smiled at him.

"Hey, Larry," said Ricky. "Do you think you might be able to teach me some kung fu?"

"Uh, I don't know, Ricky. I mean, the whole thing about kung fu is knowing when to use it. It's an **awesome responsibility**. You have to learn great self-**discipline**. It takes an inner strength. Do you know what I mean?"

"I think so," said Ricky.

As David's arm swung forward he let his hand **brush** against Tori's hand. Their hands brushed again on the backswing. As her hand came by a third time he caught hold of her last two fingers.

She didn't say a word. He didn't look at her. He didn't know if she was looking at him as he held her **pinky** and ring finger in the **palm** of his hand.

Her fingers **wiggle**d a little bit. He **loosen**ed his grip and they both shifted their hands around so that he held her entire hand.

He glanced at her and then they smiled at each other. They shifted their hands again so that their fingers **interlock**ed.

They came to the private road leading to Mrs. Bayfield's **run-down mansion**. "This is her street," **announce**d David. The sound of his own voice surprised him.

The road was cool and dark. It was lined with tall trees that **block**ed out the sun.

"It's kind of **spooky**," said Mo.

"You guys don't have to come if you"—David looked back and noticed that Larry and Mo were also holding hands— "don't want to."

"We've come this far," said Larry. "I'm not going to turn around now."

"Is she some kind of witch?" asked Ricky. He was holding Killer's **leash**.

"She put a curse on me," said David. "That's why I've been acting like such a stooge lately. It wasn't really me. It was the curse. I didn't tell you because I didn't think you'd believe me."

"I believe you," said Ricky. "I guess she put a curse on them, too," he said, **gesturing** toward Larry and Mo.

186

"No, we're just naturally weird," said Mo.

"That's why I had to get the cane," David continued. "It belongs to Felicia Bayfield. She said she'd remove the curse if I brought it back to her."

"So then what's the problem?" asked Ricky. "All you have to do is give her the cane."

"It's not that easy," said Tori. "She's a wicked, evil witch, with all kinds of strange and **mystical** powers. She might put an evil spell on all of us!" She **squeeze**d David's hand.

"I want to see her!" said Ricky.

David let go of Tori's hand and wiped his **sweat**y palm on his jeans. "Okay," he said. "Let's go."

Tori took hold of his hand again.

They slowly **approach**ed the **rust**y iron gate. David pushed it open with the cane. He and Tori walked through first, followed by Larry and Mo, then Ricky and Killer. Killer stopped and peed in the yard.

"That's the window we broke," David said quietly.

"It looks as good as new," Mo whispered.

"Someone must have fixed it," said Larry.

"Maybe," whispered Tori. "Maybe not."

"What do you mean?" asked Ricky.

"Maybe when David broke your window, her window suddenly became fixed."

"I just got a **chill** down my **spine**," said Larry.

They stepped up the wooden stairs. "That's the rocking chair," said David. They slowly approached the door. He let go of

Tori's hand.

"You have to **knock**," said Tori. "The doorbell's broken."

David opened the screen door, then turned and looked **quizzical**ly at her.

"I mean it looks broken," she said. She shrugged. "You can try it if you want."

"No, it's broken," said David. He raised the **shrunken**-head door knocker and hit it three times against the hardwood door. Then he stepped back and slowly closed the screen door so it wouldn't **bang** shut.

Tori gripped David's arm with both her hands.

"What if she's dead?" whispered Mo. "What if she died before she can remove the curse?"

"Maybe the curse died with her," said Ricky.

"No, it doesn't work that way," Larry explained. "If somebody puts a curse on you, then dies, there's no way to remove the curse. And if you have children, they'll be cursed too."

There was a **click**ing sound behind the door, then it opened a few inches. Mrs. Bayfield **peer**ed out.

"I brought back the cane," said David, holding it up for her to see.

"So you did. So you did!"

The door closed. Then the safety chain was released and the door opened wide.

Tori dropped to her knees. "Please don't hurt me," she begged. "I know you have great powers, but David Ballinger brought back the cane like he said he would, so you'll remove the curse you put on him. I just came along with David Ballinger."

Mrs. Bayfield's green eyes **dart**ed from Tori to David to Tori, then back to David. "And who, Mr. Ballinger, are these other rapscallions★ you brought?"

Still holding hands, Mo and Larry **stoop**ed down a little too. "I'm Larry and this is Mo," said Larry.

"Maureen," said Mo.

"We made him pour lemonade on his head," said Larry, trying to get on her good side.

David thought he saw Mrs. Bayfield start to smile, but her face quickly returned to its **stern** expression as she focused on Ricky. "Is that your dog?" she asked.

Ricky shook his head. "It's hers." He pointed at Mo. "I'm his brother." He pointed at David.

"I see," said Mrs. Bayfield. "Well, come inside. All of you. Bring the dog, too."

"His name's Killer," said Mo, by way of a **warn**ing.

★ rapscallion 악한, 무뢰한.

33

IT SEEMED to David that all the faces on the wall were staring at him; the man with the scar, the woman with the double **chin**, the half-man, half-lion. He tried not to look at the face of the **ordinary** man with the wire-**rim**med glasses, but his eyes kept being **drawn** to it. The man's face had a very slight smile. David didn't remember seeing that smile the last time.

Felicia Bayfield **rub**bed her long, skinny hands together. "So, Mr. Ballinger," she said. "You want me to remove the **curse**, do you?"

He **anxious**ly waited. He felt Tori **squeeze** his hand, and he squeezed back.

There was a **couch**, a love seat, and two large chairs in the living room, but he and his friends were all **bunch**ed together on the couch. Killer lay in Mo's lap.

Mrs. Bayfield sat in the chair across from them. "Well?" she demanded.

"Oh," said David. "I didn't know you wanted me to answer. I thought it was one of those questions, you know, that you're not supposed to answer."

"Rhetorical,★" whispered Tori.

"Rhetorical," said David.

"Hrrmph," muttered Mrs. Bayfield.

"He brought back the cane," said Tori. "You said you'd remove the curse if he brought back the cane."

"Silence!" ordered Mrs. Bayfield. "I don't like *children* trying to tell me what to do. In my day children were taught to respect their elders." She rose from her chair. "Stand up, Tori!" she commanded.

Tori let go of David's hand and stood up.

Mrs. Bayfield grabbed her elbow and said, "Come with me into the kitchen."

David leaped to his feet. "She didn't do anything," he said, taking hold of Tori's other arm. "She was just—"

Felicia Bayfield's cold stare silenced him. He sat back down on the couch and watched Mrs. Bayfield lead Tori through a door at the end of the room.

"What do you think she's going to do to her?" whispered Ricky.

"I wonder how she knew her name was Tori," asked Mo.

"I hope she doesn't steal her face," said Larry.

★ rhetorical 수사의문문의. 굳이 대답을 요구하는 것은 아니면서 서술이나 명령의 효과를 나타내는 의문문.

"What?" asked David.

"I hope she doesn't steal her face," Larry repeated.

"No, what were you saying, Mo?" David asked.

"Tori never said her name," said Mo. "I wonder how she knew it."

"That's just part of her powers," David explained. "She's been watching me for the last few weeks. She knows everything I do. She's seen me with Tori. Still—"

"What?" asked Mo.

"She called her Tori, but she called me Mr. Ballinger."

"So?"

"I don't know," said David. He looked at the faces on the wall. The ordinary man was no longer smiling. The face hadn't really changed, but it just didn't seem to be smiling anymore. Maybe it never was.

Larry **gasp**ed.

David turned around to see Tori step back into the living room holding a mask over her face. She was followed by Mrs. Bayfield. Each step Tori took was very slow and **deliberate**. Her hands **rigid**ly held the mask in front of her.

It was a mask of her own face.

The shape of the nose, the mouth, everything was the same. Every **freckle**.

Mrs. Bayfield was holding a glass filled with a cloudy yellow liquid. "Stop!" she commanded.

Tori stopped and stood perfectly still, like a **statue**.

Mrs. Bayfield stepped past her and held out the glass to

David. "Here."

He hesitated a moment, then took the glass.

"Drink it," she said.

For just a second he considered throwing it in her face, but that was how he got into this **mess in the first place.**

"If you want the curse to be removed," she said, "you better drink."

"What about her?" he asked.

"Only one thing can save her now," said Mrs. Bayfield.

"What?"

"First you have to drink."

He drank the liquid. It was sweet, but at the same time very **sour.**

"Ahhhhhh . . . ." said Mrs. Bayfield as if she had been the one who drank it. "I feel a lot better. We are both now rid of the **horrible** curse."

"You?" asked Mo.

"The curse was just as **painful** for me as it was for Mr. Ballinger," she said. "Maybe even worse for me."

"What about Tori?" asked David. He looked at her, rigid like a statue, her face in front of her face.

"Kiss her," said Mrs. Bayfield.

Tori seemed to move just a little bit, then became perfectly still again.

David got up from the couch and stood directly in front of her. He could feel his own **heartbeat** and he could see Tori's body **tremble** just a little bit. She had a beautiful face, even if it wasn't **attach**ed to her head.

He no longer believed any of this. Besides, he never believed in curses in the first place.

He kissed the mask gently on the lips. He was surprised by how hard and **stiff** it felt.

"Oooh." Tori **swoon**ed behind the mask. She dropped to the floor in a **faint**. Her mask still covered her.

"Okay," said David. "Now tell me what's going on."

Tori removed the mask. She still had her face behind it. She **blink**ed her eyes. "Where am I?" she asked.

"You can stop **pretend**ing," said David.

"I **assure** you, Mr. Ballinger," said Mrs. Bayfield, "no one—"

"Why do you keep calling me Mr. Ballinger?" he asked.

"That's your name."

"Except you call her Tori," he pointed out. "You two know each other. You call me Mr. Ballinger because that's what she always used to call me!"

Mrs. Bayfield and Tori looked at each other. Then they both laughed.

"What? You mean she's not a **witch**?" asked Larry.

"She's my aunt," said Tori, getting up. She hugged Felicia Bayfield and they both laughed again. "My great-aunt."

David looked at the two of them together and wondered why he hadn't noticed it sooner. They looked very much alike. If nothing else, their green eyes should have **given** it **away**. He wondered if Mrs. Bayfield used to have red hair, too.

He **glance**d at Ricky, who was still sitting **petrified** on the corner of the couch.

"We had you going," said Tori. "You thought that drink was my face juice, didn't you?"

"Oh, I knew it was lemonade all along," said David.

"Then why'd you kiss her?" asked Ricky.

He felt himself **blush** as he **shrug**ged his shoulders.

Tori also blushed. "That caught me by surprise too," she said. "I didn't know she was going to tell you to do *that*."

"Wait," said Mo. "I don't get it. If you're just a normal person, how'd you put a curse on David?"

"I never said I was a normal person," said Mrs. Bayfield.

Tori laughed.

"But no, I did not put a curse on him," she continued. She turned to David. "When you and your **compatriot**s attacked me, one of them said something like, 'Watch out, the witch might put a curse on you.' So I made up a curse. I don't even remember what I said."

"'Your Doppelgänger will **regurgitate** on your soul,'" said David.

Mrs. Bayfield laughed. "It's not very good, but I didn't have a lot of time to think of something better." She waved it off. "I had completely forgotten about it until you suddenly appeared at my door **rant**ing and **raving** about curses and lemonade and your pants falling down. I had absolutely no idea who you were or what you were talking about. And then, to my **utter astonish**ment, I realized you were one of the boys who had attacked me, and that you really believed I had put a curse on you." She held out her hands and smiled. "But I certainly didn't know you were the famous *Mr. Ballinger.*" She looked at Tori.

Tori blushed again.

"But you did know my name," said David. "And my phone number. I saw it written on a pad of paper."

"I wrote that," said Tori. "I called you from here. You probably don't remember. I heard you answer the phone and then I got scared and hung up. I just wanted to find out . . . I mean, you had been so nice to me and then you suddenly just started ignoring me. I just wanted to find out why. I thought maybe it was something I said, or maybe Maureen was your girlfriend and she didn't want you talking to me."

"Me?" **exclaim**ed Mo.

"Yeah, well, what about you and Randy?" asked David.

"That was . . . Okay, I sat next to him at the movies, but I didn't go there *with* him. It was just a **coincidence**. We shared a box of Milk Duds." She shrugged. "Is that why you stopped talking to me?"

"No. I was afraid of the curse," explained David. "Larry had a plan to remove the curse." He glanced at Larry. "We tried it, and then we had to wait three days to see if it worked. I was afraid to talk to you during those three days. I guess I acted kind of **weird**. But that night you called me, I was going to call you, except I didn't know your phone number."

"Oh," said Tori, disappointed he hadn't called. "I wasn't home anyway. I was here."

"So that's why you poured lemonade on your head!" exclaimed Ricky. "That was *Larry's plan*."

"You got a better one?" asked Larry.

"Did you say David's pants fell down?" Mo asked Mrs. Bayfield.

"He has the cutest purple shorts!" exclaimed Tori. She and Mo laughed.

"You said you closed your eyes!" said David.

"I lied."

"I assure you, David," said Mrs. Bayfield. "If I'd known you'd come back with your face so badly **bruised**, I would never have asked you to bring me my cane. I'm very sorry about that."

"Me too," said Tori. "I didn't know what to do when you said you had to fight Roger. I didn't know how to stop you. And then he just kept hitting you over and over." She **shivered**.

David shrugged. He was glad he'd brought back the cane, even if there was no curse. He was glad he **stood up to** Roger, too.

He had gotten his face back. So what if it was a little bruised? At least he could feel it was there.

34

"YOU SEE that mask there," said Tori, pointing at the face of the **ordinary** man with the wire-**rim**med glasses. "That's Herbert Bayfield. She made that for him on their twenty-fifth wedding anniversary."

"Wow," said Mo. "He looks so real."

"She's actually a very famous artist," Tori **brag**ged. "She's got masks hanging in museums all over the world. One museum **offer**ed her a lot of money for Uncle Herbert's mask, but she won't **part** with it. It's famous for its smile that seems to appear and disappear depending on how you look at it. It's been **compare**d to the smile on the *Mona Lisa*."

"Do you think she'll make a mask of me?" asked Mo.

Tori **shrug**ged. "She looks for interesting faces. But I never know what makes a face interesting to her. Course, she also makes masks of everyone in our family." She looked at her own mask, still on the floor. "It's actually not finished yet," she said.

"That's why it was still in her studio." She picked it up and held it next to her own face. "See, it doesn't have all the **freckles**."

"Did she **count** your freckles first?" asked David.

"Huh?" Tori smiled. "No. You can't count them because some are so light it's hard to tell if they're really even freckles. That's why she's such a good artist. She can do all that."

Mrs. Bayfield returned from the kitchen with cookies, a **pitcher** of lemonade, and some glasses. "Would anyone like some face juice?" she asked.

She poured everyone a glass.

"What about you both saying I looked like a Greek **poet**?" asked David.

"What?" asked Felicia Bayfield.

"We went to the foreign film festival last weekend," Tori explained. "There was a movie about a Greek poet. You were dressed just like him."

"Was it a Greek movie?" asked Mo.

"No, it was French," said Tori. "But it was about a Greek poet."

"Oh, yeah, I think I saw it when I lived in France," said Larry.

"Is that somewhere near Indianapolis?" asked David.

Larry **ignore**d him.

"Okay," said Mo. "How about this? Maybe you thought you were just making up some words, but maybe you happened to say the words just right and really did put a curse on David without even knowing it."

"That means he's still cursed," said Larry. "And you don't know how to remove it."

"How else do you explain all the things that happened to him?" asked Mo.

"Tell me more about this curse," said Tori's famous aunt.

"I don't know," said David. "I've never believed in anything like that, but it was just so **weird**. Everything that those guys did to you happened to me. There were too many **coincidences**."

He told her everything that happened, from breaking his parents' bedroom window to his pants falling down. He even told her about the **flour** falling on his head.

"Well," said Mrs. Bayfield, "I have an idea. But I don't know if it's right."

"What?" asked Tori.

"If you are cursed, Mr. Ballinger—David," said Mrs. Bayfield, "it is only because you are a **sensitive**, caring human being."

"Him?" asked Larry with a laugh.

"I imagine David felt very **guilt**y about what he and the other boys did to me. Didn't you, David?"

"I thought you were just a lonely old lady," said David. "I didn't know you were famous."

Mrs. Bayfield smiled. "You probably felt you should have been **punish**ed for what you did," she said. "And when nobody punished you, you punished yourself."

"You mean I broke our window on purpose?"

"You or your **subconscious**."

200

"And I purposely didn't tie my pants tight enough because I wanted them to fall down?"

"'Fraid so."

David shook his head. "I'm really weird, aren't I? I mean Roger and Randy and Scott didn't punish themselves."

"They **obvious**ly are not as sensitive as you are." Mrs. Bayfield smiled warmly at David. "You're a caring, **thoughtful, considerate** human being. Maybe that is a curse in this cold world we live in. You have the soul of a poet."

Tori **beam**ed at him.

David looked at all the faces on the wall. Little did he know that someday his face would be up there with them.

35

DAVID THOUGHT a lot about what Tori's aunt had said. He really never did believe one hundred percent that he was **curse**d. But **on the other hand** he also found it hard to believe that he did all that **stuff** to himself on purpose.

Or maybe his **subconscious** did it to him.

Or his Doppelgänger.

But why else would he **flip off** his mother if he didn't want to get **punish**ed? Then his mother didn't even punish him for that, he remembered, so he had to keep punishing himself.

In the end, he realized, all he had to do was tell Felicia Bayfield he was sorry. The whole time his subconscious, or Doppelgänger, kept doing stuff to him, trying to make him do that. At last he didn't tie his pants tight enough and that finally did it. He ran to tell her he was sorry and the curse never **struck** again.

Or, on the other hand, Mrs. Bayfield could be wrong and

he still might be cursed. Or maybe that was just what life was all about. Maybe everyone is cursed, **one way or another**. He remembered Larry and Mo saying that they sometimes felt like there was a curse on them too. Everyone steps in dogshit once in a while.

It was like Mrs. Bayfield said: We all try to act like we're so important—doctors, lawyers, artists—but really we know that at any moment our pants might fall down.

The bell rang. David walked out of math, put his books away in his locker, and headed out for **recess**.

He felt himself **tense** up when he saw Roger and Scott heading toward him even though they had pretty much stopped **bother**ing him. Scott had his arm around Ginger.

I guess not everyone's cursed, David realized. Scott Simpson didn't seem like he was cursed at all. He always got everything he wanted. He was popular. He got all A's. He was a good **athlete**. He was handsome. It **hardly** seemed fair.

Scott walked by without even glancing at his former best friend.

But then again, thought David, Scott Simpson didn't have the soul of a **poet**.

He checked to make sure his **fly** was zipped, then headed out to join his friends.

"DID YOU see what David gave me?" asked Tori. "He made it in shop class."

"His apple-cheese board!" exclaimed Mo.

"It's not an apple-cheese board," said Tori, somewhat **offend**ed. "It's a heart."

"Oh, uh, that's right," Mo said very quickly. "It's a heart. I don't know why I said it was an apple."

"I think it looks more like an apple," said Larry. "Not the kind of apples you get in here in America, but the kind of apples I ate when I lived in Zambia."

150 years later . . .

36

"HERE COMES the drooble!" said Harley.

His buddies laughed.

Willy tried to **ignore** them.

"What's the matter, drooble?" asked Harley. "Your underwear too tight?"

Harley's friends laughed again, and so did a couple of girls.

Willy **redden**ed. At least he didn't hear Maria laugh. He would have recognized her laugh. It was almost musical.

"No **quack**ing," said Mrs. Po, his teacher. "We are in a museum, not a quack factory."

Everyone stopped talking. They were on a field **trip**. It was March 15, 2139. There was no school tomorrow because it was David Ballinger's birthday.

"Hey, drooble!"

Willy turned around to see Quentin **flip him off**. He looked away and focused his **attention** on the painting at the end of the hall. It was a picture of a man with a bucket over his head.

Everyone in his class laughed when they saw it. "What a drooble!" someone said.

"We should get a bucket for Willy," said Quentin. "He's so ugly!"

Willy entered the Bayfield room. He looked at all the faces on the walls. He moved from mask to mask until he got to the face of David Ballinger. Then he stopped and **stare**d.

I **bet** nobody ever called you a drooble, he thought.

Everyone in his class had had to **memorize** a famous speech. Willy had chosen Ballinger's Moscow Address. He remembered how important he felt as he stood and **recite**d it in front of the class. Maria's eyes seemed to shine at him as he spoke with the **dignity** and **grace** that made Ballinger famous.

He was still standing in front of the mask when Maria stepped up beside him. He was afraid to even look at her. His heart was **pound**ing so loudly he was afraid she might hear it. He **grip**ped the wood bar in front of the **exhibit**.

They stood next to each other without saying anything for several minutes, both staring at the face of David Ballinger.

She started to go.

"Hi, Maria," he said, then **blush**ed.

It was so stupid. He should have said hi when she first got there, not when she was leaving! When someone leaves you're supposed to say bye, but he couldn't say bye without having first said hi to her. *I'm such a drooble!*

"Hi, Willy," she replied.

He watched her brown ponytail **bounce** behind her as she walked out of the room. "Bye," he **whisper**ed.

He looked back up at the mask of David Ballinger. *I wish I could be more like you.*